SEMAPHORE

By
J. Randolf Scott

All characters in this book are fictitious.
Any resemblance to real persons, either living or dead
is purely coincidental.

The cover picture shows a modern fibre optic lamp.
These fibres are about the same size as the filaments
used by Edward Raine, about six times thicker than
human hair.

DEDICATION

To my two sons Julian and John

PREFACE

Mater artium necessitas.

Necessity is the mother of invention.

CONTENTS

INTRODUCTION.

Most of the detail in this book is derived from the 'Workshop Notebook', which was later renamed the 'Optics Notebook' written by Edward B. Raine, circa 1814 shortly after he joined the company of Ayres and Compton in Leadenhall Street in the city of London. Understandably, much of the detail is technical in nature, with very little personal material, which is what we should expect from this type of journal. The Notebook is not very revealing about private matters or opinions, except for the odd cryptic comment here and there, which prompts me to imagine or surmise much of what went on from day to day, based on the prevailing attitudes, morals and prejudices of the times. It was a notebook, not a diary. However, small details do occur from time to time, that reveal something about the man himself.

I have taken appropriate extracts from the Notebook (in script) to illustrate my narrative in normal text.

The 1740 survey of the Norwood area does not show the cart track known as Coppice Lane, where the Raine and Jessop families lived. Nor does this survey mention the two farms or small-holdings. However, the survey does show the coppice or area of woodland, roughly situated at the top of what is now Landsdown Hill, off Knights Hill. Obviously considerable building developments have occurred since those days.

Although Edward doesn't say so directly, we can assume that the two farms, Coppice Farm and Spring Farm were established after 1740, as tenant small-holdings or market gardens, with Lord Thurlow as the landowner. Edward hints that the farm-houses were built by his father, George, and his neighbour Harold Jessop from local chert. We also know that the houses were thatched originally because Edward mentions converting the roof to tiles. We know too that spring water was available to both farms. It is most likely that somewhere close by there was a natural spring, which the two farmers diverted to cisterns nearer their respective houses.

We have no details of how big the farms were, but we do know that Harold Jessop kept cattle because Edward tells us fresh milk was available every day. Edward also tells us that his father grew a variety of vegetables for home consumption, and that his father sold fresh fruit, mainly cherries, apples and pears in season at the local market, as well as strawberries, blackberries and crab apples, because they commanded a good price at market. Apparently, there was little money to be made from arable crops, although some land was put to oats for home use. Edward also tells us that his mother baked fresh bread, probably daily. In hard times the field was sown with wheat for bread.

We have little information about where Edward's parents, George and Ann, originated. They are certainly not listed in the local parish records of the time. We don't even know when they moved to the Lower Norwood area and there are no birth records of either Edward or his elder brother, Thomas. It seems that they were born elsewhere.

Edward gives us no clues as to where he went to school at any level, but he does hint that he was educated at a college, prior to becoming an apprentice clock maker, probably at the age of 14 or 15. We do know that he was very well educated because of his wide knowledge. We know too that he was well versed in mathematics. Edward doesn't mention who he was originally apprenticed to, but he does refer to his time working for Cummings. There is no mention of how well his brother, Thomas, was educated other than he joined the Navy, probably as a cabin boy at the age of 14 and that he was killed in November 1794 in a battle with the French, off the coast of France, while serving aboard HMS Alexander under Rear Admiral Richard Bligh. Edward says that his brother had the rank of midshipman at the time of his death.

Edward probably used the British Museum, which at that time was located at Montague House, frequently to research new ideas, but his journal only refers to the Museum once. Whilst we would all like to know more about the intriguing Edward Raine, the only remnant that we have is his Workshop Notebook, which is hardly a biography; more of a laboratory notebook, that was probably written to protect his prior knowledge against possible future Patent claims.

THE COMPANY

Edward doesn't tell us whether he joined Cummings as an apprentice and served his time there, or whether his did his apprenticeship elsewhere and started with Cummings as a freeman. Alexander Cumming, had been in business in Bond Street long enough for Edward to have served his apprenticeship there, but we cannot be sure.

Back in 1763 Cumming had acquired a considerable reputation as a clockmaker. He was appointed a member of the Admiralty commission, to adjudicate on John Harrison's nautical chronometer, which would allow ships to calculate their longitude position with great accuracy.

Harrison eventually won the £10,000 prize money, offered by the Admiralty, for his clock, but had difficulty getting his money from the notoriously slow paying Admiralty and had to appeal to the King to get his money. It was a condition of the competition that the drawings and designs remained the property of the Admiralty.

Cumming also made a recording barograph for King George III. He also wrote books about watch and clock works, and about the effect on roads of carriage wheels with rims of various shapes. In 1770 he is credited with the invention of the microtome, a machine for making extremely thin slices as used in microscope slide-preparation.

In 1775 he made a major advance on the design of the flushing toilet that included the concept of a water trap within the pan, which nowadays is called an 'S' bend or a 'P' bend, that prevents foul smells from re-entering the house.

With his brother, Cumming was involved in the development of the Pentonville district of London, where he had a house and an organ shop.

In 1783 Cumming was a joint founder of the Royal Society of Edinburgh and was made a Fellow. He died on 8 March 1814, in Pentonville, and the business died with him. It was under Cumming that Edward gained much of his experience with various precision machines not just clocks.

Edward joined Jeremiah Ayres and Oliver Compton in April 1814. He was already acquainted with Ayres and Compton from his time at Cummings, but not on a personal level. It was Oliver Compton who advised him to apply for his present job, because Compton knew that the firm was short of expertise with mechanisms and accurate metalwork.

Jeremiah Ayres was a time served glass worker and lens grinder. He worked for several other instrument makers, including George Adams Senior, before starting his own company with Oliver Compton, a cabinet-maker. Ayres was a Quaker, but Edward does not mention whether Compton had any particular religious persuasion other than being a Christian.

Ayres was the senior partner and it was he who frowned upon advertising. His motto was 'let the product speak for itself'. The firm only undertook sub-contract work to other instrument makers. Most of their products were re-labelled under the name of the main contractor. The firm had a very good reputation for excellent craftsmanship and high-quality standards. However, it was Compton who really understood the importance of presentation. Their clients rarely understood or could use the instruments that Ayres and Compton made, so the initial impact of the presentation box was crucial to making a sale, hence Ayres collaboration with Compton, a skilled cabinet-maker. The polish, finish and quality of the fit of the box joints were as important as the instrument itself. Much of their contract work came from Christopher Steadman, also in Leadenhall Street, who in turn obtained much of his work from George Adams. The instrument makers of London all knew each other and inter-traded frequently.

Often the degree of accuracy required by a contract was beyond the capacity of some manufacturers, who turned to other more specialised instrument makers, such as Ayres and Compton. Indeed, the sign outside the workshop in Leadenhall Street proclaimed that Ayres and Compton were precision workers in wood, metals and glass. There was no mention of Instrument Making, although in practice that was their business. They were, what we would nowadays call, sub-contractors to the trade. They were not even listed as instrument makers in the Trade Directories of the time. Both Ayres and Compton were widely known and respected in the trade. In effect the two partners were the principal salesmen who obtained business through their many contacts in the trade rather than knocking on doors or touting for clients amongst wealthy gentlemen of the day.

Periodically, other instrument makers would re-direct inventors and clients to Ayres and Compton to consult with Edward. Word soon got around, that Edward was a good, sound arbiter with respect to assessing whether an invention or idea was worth pursuing and whether it could be made to work. Even within the company, Edward was always the man who came up with solutions to problems, and in a short time he was elevated to the post of Chief Designer and General Works Manager. In effect, it was Edward who ran the firm on a day-to-day basis, with popular assent from all the employees.

If the firm was awarded a lucrative contract by a principal instrument-maker, it was customary for the two partners to present the principal with a gift of recognition. Again, it was Edward who came up with the idea of exquisitely made snuff-boxes, crafted from rare and exotic woods, with a properly engineered brass container inside. Originally, these boxes were made by apprentices as a test piece to measure their skills, but they proved so popular that it became a lucrative business on its own account. It was this enterprise that acquainted Edward with 'French Polish' and the unique properties of shellac. Normally, French polishing was outrageously expensive, but machine buffing provided a much quicker and cheaper way to achieve equivalent results. Later, these 'gifts' were extended to cigar humidors, which were so well made that it was virtually impossible to see the joints in the boxes.

Ayres and Compton were not the only instrument makers to branch out to the public in general, particularly in periods of peace when government ordinance contracts diminished. As a result, many middle-class homes came to possess thermometers and barometers, housed in decorative wooden cases, where previously such instruments were exclusively the possessions of the gentry.

Edward was intensely loyal by nature, not only to his employers, but also to his fellow employees: their welfare was his welfare too, although his attitude to workers welfare was out-of-step with common practice of the times. Until the arrival of Edward, the two partners kept the firm's books, which by all accounts was common for those times. As general manager, Edward needed to know what was in the forward order book and how much the firm was owed by their customers. He didn't think the partners were intentionally secretive, but clearly this information was not known to him, which prevented him from planning effectively. He was the self-elected problem solver for the company, and this was just another problem to be solved, although not a technical problem.

Workshop Notebook
Edward B. Raine

Monday, 11 April 1814
Started work as mechanical designer for A & C. Greeted by partners. Introduced to workers, V. friendly – good men. Good b/fast oats and fruit preserves. Feel good. High class cabinet work. Lens grinding. Metal working machines good condition. Financial state of firm secret. Planning non-existent. Need proper book keeper urgent.

His solution was quite simple: he had to persuade the partners that the firm had an excellent reputation for high quality workmanship, and for producing goods on time. To do this consistently, the firm needed to employ a professional book-keeper to maintain their reputation for professionalism in their products. Edward claimed that he was against the idea of increasing the wage bill with a non-productive person, but he firmly believed that a good book-keeper could easily earn their keep by recovering long standing debts alone. He then proposed the idea of employing a woman to do this task because female book-keepers could be hired at half the price of a man. Later, Edward discovered that neither partner liked keeping the accounts; it was a tedious and onerous task. Worse still, both the partners admitted to being reluctant about asking for payment, which suggested that a considerable sum of outstanding debt was owed to the company. Little wonder that both partners agreed to Edward's suggestion, particularly when he guaranteed that the book-keeper would more than pay her way.

THE BOOK-KEEPER

Tuesday, 19 April 1814

Printed vacancy notice, for book-keeper. Went around coffee shops to look for applicants, yesterday. Interview with 4 persons today.

Mr Selby no good, mental arithmetic poor, untidy. Self-important.

Miss Bennet. V pretty, well dressed. No experience, poor arithmetic. Poor spelling. Gossipy, Not good enough.

Miss Thornton (Sybil). Plain, smartly dressed. Excellent arithmetic, School teacher, Superb English and grammar. Little experience but knows bookkeeping principles. Will not take no for answer. Best so far.

Mr Stoneham. Smartly dressed. Has stammer, little experience, cannot spell, good arithmetic. Too difficult to work with.

Edward advertised with a printed pamphlet in the coffee houses and taverns, even though he knew they were almost exclusively the haunt of men. He hoped that women would eventually overhear men talking about the unusual vacancy. He interviewed several prospective applicants, both men and women. However, it was Miss Sybil Thorton, formerly a school teacher, who captured his attention most. Her application letter was beautifully written and expertly constructed, which gave Edward the information he needed in a clear and concise manner. Likewise, during her interview, she was equally clear and concise. Most of all, there was something about her manner, perhaps reminiscent of her school-teaching years, which conveyed the impression that she would not tolerate excuses or equivocation. She wasn't aggressive or threatening, but it was clear that she wouldn't accept no for an answer. Edward made sure that she fully understood that she would be dealing with confidential financial matters and that to breach this confidence would mean instant dismissal.

In appearance she looked smartly and soberly dressed, with her hair drawn back in a tight bun. She was perhaps in her middle thirties, but her stern features and spectacles made her look older. Edward considered that she looked plain, rather than unattractive He also assured her that she would have his full support before offering the job to her. At first, she was speechless, but after composing herself she assured Edward that she would pay her way and that he would never regret his decision. She said this with such sincerity that Edward knew in his heart that he had made the right choice.

Promptly at 8:00 am the following day, Sybil arrived at the works to commence her duties. Edward summoned the employees and introduced Sybil to them and warned them not to swear or to be disrespectful to Sybil. He also reminded them that their wages depended on Sybil doing her job properly. As a temporary arrangement, Sybil would share his office until the carpenters could

18

build her an office of her own. Once the workers had dispersed, Edward introduced her to the partners upstairs. In their presence she made it abundantly clear that she understood the confidential nature of the work that she would be doing, and nothing related to the finances of the business would pass her lips. I suspect that they were convinced by her sincerity, just as Edward had been.

Without further ado, she set about the partners and requested to see the current books as well as any unpaid invoices and other scraps of paper relating to work done for others. She was back in her school-teacher mode, which probably accounted for the haste shown by the partners in handing over all the paperwork that they could lay hands on. Back in Edward's office Sybil commented that the books were in a dreadful state, and that she intended to copy them all into a set of new ledgers. Edward suggested that she should accompany him to the nearest stationers to purchase a complete set of good quality ledgers and journals, which he paid for from his own pocket. He noticed with some pride that Sybil took the receipt for the purchase and told him that he would be reimbursed.

About half way through the morning Sybil asked about the privy facilities, and about what the other employees did about food and refreshment. Edward cursed himself inwardly for not anticipating this problem and suggested that she should use the closet used by the partners because that was the only closet with locks. He promised to speak to the carpenters about providing a private closet for herself. He also informed her that the other employees usually brought their own food and drink.

Later that day, Sybil made a suggestion, which she pointed out was not a complaint, concerning the provision of fresh water, and possibly milk and bread for the employees. It wasn't a suggestion or a complaint, but to Edward it sounded more like an edict. He had toyed with a similar idea himself, so he wasn't disturbed by the suggestion. Instead he was encouraged by her bluntness. His customers were in for a surprise when Sybil confronts them.

Within two months of starting work, Sybil had transformed the accounts and the quantity of information they revealed. Edward felt more like a helmsman steering the ship rather than being at the mercy of the wind and waves. Most of all, the bank balance reflected Sybil's efforts to collect the outstanding debts. The improvement in the firm's finances enabled Edward to persuade the partners to invest in a small steam engine (from Henry Maudsley) to provide power to the whole works. It was he who designed and constructed better woodworking machines and better metal working lathes, drills and shapers. Systematically, Edward went through the equipment and processes used by the craftsmen, and where possible adapted them all to use steam power. This did not diminish or devalue the skills of the craftsmen and artisans. Instead it allowed them to produce more with greater consistency, as well as increasing their wages.

With the aid of a local lawyer, Sybil also instituted a printed leaflet with the firm's standard terms and conditions of contract. The most important item in these small print terms was the ninety days credit limit for repayment. It was rare within the trade, at that time, to draw up legal contracts. Instead a handwritten 'agreement' was usually signed by both parties, which normally covered the limits and responsibilities of both parties, over and above the printed conditions.

Friday, 24 June 1814
(S) has taken over completely. New printed terms and conditions. Credit limit set at 90 days. Most past debts collected. Bank account looks good. Planning meetings every Monday. Can now see ahead. V popular asset. Organised midday refreshment for workshop. New privy installed for (S). Unstoppable. Knows what confidential means. Tea served every morning. Steam engine arrived from Maudsley. Worried about explosions. Wise decision to put furnace and boiler outside in yard. Workers excited about steam powered machines. Mr A and Mr C spend all the time in coffee shops.

The general atmosphere throughout the works was buoyant. Sybil kept her word and mentioned nothing, but the arrival of the steam engine and other improvements spoke volumes about the financial health of the business. The provision of fresh spring water, bread and milk every day for all the employees confirmed that the firm was in good health and intended to keep its employees in the same way. Sybil responded to this new regime by making tea for Edward, morning and afternoon, paid for from her own pocket. At least she started paying from her own pocket until Edward found out and insisted that the firm should compensate her. She continued this routine even after she moved into her own office. The partners revelled in the new prosperity and the relief from the arduous task of keeping the accounts. The company was now running like well-oiled clockwork even without their presence, which allowed them to spend even more time in the local coffee shops discussing trends with others in the trade.

Edward insisted that the partners and Sybil should join him every morning on his tour of the works to check on the progress of each job in hand, and to check out any impending problems. In this way, everybody was kept in the picture with respect to what was happening. It was also good for morale, but most of all it infused a sense of urgency about each job. Nothing escaped the attention of the morning inspection and the employees knew it. They also knew that the informality allowed them to speak their minds and voice any complaints.

FAMILY LOSSES

It must have about this time that Edward's father was struck down with a mysterious illness after an accident with a scythe, which the local doctor diagnosed as blood poisoning. Later, when muscular spasms occurred, the doctor revised his diagnosis as lockjaw. Eventually, George's breathing became more difficult until eventually, George died. It is most likely that he died of tetanus.

Wednesday, 14 September 1814
Father died today, has been ill all week. Cut finger on scythe. Doctor says lockjaw. Spasms and difficulty breathing. Looked deathly pale. Mother distraught.

Young Edward was reminded again of the fortitude of women. Edward had no illusions about the role and position of women at that time. For centuries man had played the dominant role and had organised society in such as way as to perpetuate this state-of-affairs. Women in general had been relegated to second-class citizens: they were denied equality in every aspect of life and moreover it was enshrined in law. It is fair to say that Edward considered that women were the equal of men, even the Bible said so, although the notebook doesn't mention this view specifically. His views were obviously coloured by his love and respect for his own mother, particularly at the time of his father's death.

In terms of intellect, women were a match for any man, in Edward's opinion. Perhaps historically women were not so prevalent as men in science and philosophy, but this had more to do with opportunity rather than ability. Sybil was a good example of this. She had been a school-teacher previously, but only because that was one of the few professions open to her. Edward had opened a whole new world for her, and he had no doubts that she would excel in her new role.

Monday 19 September 1814
Decided farm was too much for mother to handle. Leased land to Jessops. Rent will help mother. Mother not looking good. Devastated by death of father. My moods are v.dark. Difficult to concentrate. Not sleeping well. Pull self together or work will suffer. Thatch roof not safe enough for mother. Asked builder to lay tiles instead.

Edward must have known that he couldn't run the farm and carry on with his own career, and promptly decided to lease the land to his neighbour Harold, except for the orchard. It would provide a steady income for his mother and relieve her of the onerous task of running the farm. Despite this, it soon became apparent that his mother had been devastated by George's death. It robbed her of the will to live, and she gradually began attacks of severe melancholy. According to his notebook, Edward himself had problems maintaining his focus, and attempting to cope with the loss of his father, which was further compounded by the deterioration of his mother. Edward was always very safety aware and overly cautious, which probably accounts for his decision to change the thatched roof of the farmhouse and replace it with tiles. Just over a year later, his mother also passed away in her sleep.

Friday, 20 October 1815
Mother died in her sleep. Never recovered from death of father. She is safe with him in heaven. I am in deep grief and shock. More than when father died. Very black moods. Brain has stopped working. Lacking confidence. Cannot wait to return to normal. Frightened by prospect of permanent melancholy.

Edward took the loss of his mother more seriously than the death of his father. His notebook refers to 'black moods', and a marked decline in his ability to analyse problems and come up with innovative solutions. At the same time, he must have inherited his mother's fortitude because his 'black moods' faded, and he regained his usual confidence. Perhaps it was the result of his decision to employ a live-in house-keeper, Elsie Hopkins. I dare say that Sybil may have had a hand in this decision, but the notebook gives no clues. The presence of a woman in his house again may have tipped the balance. It is sufficient to say that Edward was back to himself again in a few months.

Tuesday 5 December 1815
Decided to take on housekeeper. Elsie Hopkins. E.H. young, healthy, of slight frame but strong, good cook, polite, quiet, mild tempered, cheerful, plain featured, soberly dressed.

Not surprisingly, the notebook only has a brief reference to young Elsie, "E.H. young, healthy, of slight frame but strong, good cook, polite, quiet, mild tempered, cheerful, plain featured, soberly dressed".

THE SHUTTER TELEGRAPH

Friday 15 March 1816
Coffee shop gossip – shutter telegraph dismantled in May last year. Parliament agreed new semaphore telegraph to Portsmouth. Visited Museum library to get more details. Never heard of it before. Vaguely recall French system of levered semaphores. Flawed idea because open for all to see (CYPHER). New Admiralty method by Vice Admiral Popham, similar to French. Trial line to Chatham starts 1816. New Portsmouth line by 1822. What are the navy doing in the meantime? Line of sight and telescopes not practical at 5 miles. Depends on visibility and weather. Daylight only. Not good enough. Bad decision. Must be a better way. Messages must be coded for secrecy.

About two years after Edward first started at the firm, he happened to overhear some coffee shop gossip about a new permanent semaphore line between London and Portsmouth would be built to replace the now closed 'shutter line' which had only just been dismantled in May 1815 after victory against the French at Waterloo. This was the Admiralty's response to the perceived possibility of yet another invasion threat from France, or perhaps the possibility of another war with America, even though the Treaty of Ghent had only just been signed. Edward was not in the least interested in the political motives behind the decision by the Admiralty:

it was the prospect of a long-term lucrative contract that attracted him.

Edward spent a productive day in the British Museum reading room at Montague House, finding out more about the original semaphore line, because he had never come across it before and didn't even realize that it ever existed.

His journal contains a series of short notes about the salient features of this device. The original shutter telegraph network was created in 1795, no doubt inspired by the success of the French system built by the Chappe brothers in 1792. The British method was based on an idea by Lord George Murray, which used six rotating shutters on a twenty-foot high frame. There were three lines constructed; the first was from the Admiralty in London sending messages east to the dockyard at Sheerness and to Deal, which opened in January 1796. The second, was a very long line, southwards from London to the naval station at Portsmouth, and then west to Plymouth facing the Atlantic Ocean. This line opened in May 1806. The third line worked eastwards to Yarmouth and commenced working in June 1808. All three were abandoned in 1814 once the Bonaparte regime in France had been defeated.

The British telegraph system was a pale shadow compared to the comprehensive system devised by the

French engineer, Claude Chappe and his brothers, who succeeded in covering France with a network of 556 stations stretching a total distance of 3000 miles.

Edward also notes that the French were using 'levered Semaphores' situated on towers nine to ten miles apart and were able to send messages over hundreds of miles at around 1.75 words per minute. Although this was very fast compared to horse and rider, in Edward's opinion the sending rate ought to be around 2 to 3 secs per character. The practical message rate would depend on whether a codebook was used or not. Code words could consist of single characters whereas readable text would on average involve five characters per word, i.e. five times longer.

The word CYPHER also appears after this comment, which suggests that Edward was already thinking about ways to make messages more secure, because the semaphores were plainly visible to anyone.

The system in both countries relied on line of sight operation using men with telescopes, which attracted the comment from Edward that this is unworkable. Edward also comments that Bonaparte was totally secure in his own country, so why did he venture to Waterloo, which was outside the protection of his telegraph network?

Edward was shocked to discover that the original British system was only fully operational for one-fifth of the year, because it was regularly interrupted by fog, and even by rain or gloomy weather. He comments again in his notebook that this is useless and unacceptable.

The Admiralty almost immediately regretted the loss of the telegraph, and by 1815 had obtained permission of Parliament to build the new Semaphore Telegraph system; securing peacetime powers to acquire property and prevent obstruction of the signals. It adopted the semaphore apparatus of the newly appointed Rear-Admiral Sir Home Riggs Popham, which had two rotating arms, rather than swinging shutters. An experimental telegraph line from London to Chatham dockyard, was commenced in 1816. The intent was to use the new semaphore method on the proposed line from London to Portsmouth. If successful, then an extension would be built to distant Plymouth.

The proposed new method consisted of a vertical mast set thirty feet above station-houses on high ground, about 5 miles apart, within sight of each other; requiring constant, eye-straining vigilance by the signalmen in the daylight hours.

Edward concludes that the Admiralty were about to make a serious and costly mistake, simply because they were, virtually, duplicating the previous unacceptable method. He knew that his forte was creating innovative solutions to problems, and here was an example just waiting for him to solve. The new semaphore line was planned to be operational in seven years, which inspired him to come up with an immediate plan. It was plain to him that his solution would have to offer; immunity from the weather or visibility, day and night operation, fewer stations and fewer operators to reduce the capital and running costs.

INSPIRATION

Tuesday, 2 April 1816
Best basis is French model because it works. 10-mile intervals – again similar to French method – half the building costs. Use women as operators – half the cost again. Telescopes not practical. What else?

Edward's initial concept was based on a simplified version of the French model, simply because he knew it worked. However, he was keenly aware of its shortcomings and the huge cost of building and manning the semaphore towers or stations. He arbitrarily defined the distance between stations as ten miles, perhaps because it was roughly the same as the French system, or perhaps it was exactly twice the new Admiralty telegraph distance. At a stroke he had halved the capital cost and the running cost. If he used women operators, then he could halve the running costs again.

Tuesday, 9 April 1816
No telescopes – direct vision only. Signals not visible at 10 miles. Gunpowder flash is visible, but tower needs to be very high – curvature of Earth. No solution in sight.

There are signs in his notebook that some days must have passed before Edward made the next entry:' no telescopes – direct vision only'. In effect he was ruling out the use of telescopes, probably because he was convinced that it was impractical to expect people to maintain vigilance for long periods whilst looking through telescope lenses. The delay in making this comment was probably because he recognised that at ten miles apart, the signalling arms would hardly be visible. It was an intractable dilemma. If he already had any ideas, then we could expect his notebook to reveal them regardless of how tentative they may have been.

Monday, 22 April 1816
Possible eye strain with very strong lights – sunlight. Still no solution.

Yet more time passed by before Edward made more comments in his notebook, related to observing very powerful and bright lights by observers for long periods and the possible effects on eyesight. It is clear from the notebook that Edward's strategy was to apply practical, logical and disciplined analysis to a problem, rather than out-of-the-blue inspiration: the stuff of genius. Edward was gradually defining the parameters of the problem.

Unfortunately for Edward, he was ahead of his time. Within a matter of a few years, in the early 1820s Goldsworthy Gurney discovered that lime pellets would burn with intense incandescence if heated to around 2500 degrees Celsius with an oxy-hydrogen blowpipe. By 1826 a Scottish surveyor, Thomas Drummond, had built a practical version of limelight that was used to survey the Highlands. Apparently, Drummond's light could be seen an astonishing 68 miles away. Edward knew none of this: the only light available to him was sunlight or the Argand lamp. Obviously, later on, Edward did investigate whether he could harness the brilliance of limelight, but eventually discarded the idea because it involved generating significant quantities of pure oxygen, which at that time was no easy task. Commercial quantities of gas in steel 'bottles' did not become available until towards the end of the century. In effect, limelight was little more than a laboratory curiosity. The gas 'mantle' (a fabric sleeve impregnated with rare earth oxides) had much greater potential, but even that was still half a century away

However, it was common knowledge to men of science at the time, that calcium hydroxide (lime) would glow if heated in a normal gas flame. Edward even records several experiments with heating lime with coal gas and compressed air. No doubt this was inspired by the knowledge that he could supply his more remote signalling stations with containers of these compressed gases, rather than trying to produce gases locally. Edward was always driven by practicalities.

Friday, 3 May 1816
End of week experiment to make Argand lamp brighter with
compressed air. Partial success, but not good enough. Works
better with smoky flame. Pure oxygen with oil lamp works well
– about same as lime in coal gas.

The notebook also records that Edward attempted to improve the brightness of the Argand lamp flame by burning the wick in pure oxygen. It appears that this idea was quite successful, but again Edward dismissed the idea, simply because oxygen gas was not freely available. Possibly, Edward didn't feel confident enough to dabble with chemistry: his inclination was engineering. However, he did note that the flame brightness depended on the type of oil being burnt, and that smoky flames were generally brighter. He also notes that the addition of compressed air to assist in the total combustion of the lamp oil does not make the flame brighter, as does oxygen. Edward concludes that burning oil in pure oxygen and the glow of lime heated by coal gas and air (not incandescent lime-light) are of similar brightness. In practical terms oxygen was not a realistic option.

Monday 6 May 1816
Nothing can compete with sunlight. Not enough in England.
What about night time? Even sunlight not always visible in
poor weather.

The most significant observation that he made at this time was that no lamp or device is likely to be brighter than the sun, and even sunlight cannot always penetrate poor visibility. Therefore, his efforts would be best diverted towards solving this problem first, rather than pointless experiments with sources of light that will never compare with sunlight. Obviously for night time signals usage, a bright light source would be needed, but that was a problem for another time.

Despite Edward's systematic analysis, his mind had been infected by his prior knowledge of the British and French semaphore systems, which he was intent on improving. He overlooked the fact that any form of semaphore is a means of transmitting several elements of information wrapped up in a single image. His immediate response was to convert the information elements into individual beams of light and to transmit these beams separately instead of using flags or signalling arms. Later, in 1840 Samuel Finley Breese Morse was faced with the identical problem when he brilliantly co-invented the Morse code, which allowed a single cable (electric or optical) to carry messages by representing letters of the alphabet by dots and dashes.

Monday 13 May 1816
2 semaphore flags in 8 positions round the clock need 16 beams of light. Alphabet and numerals only need 5 beams (32 combinations). Numerals, 0 to 9 are A to J plus numeric switch. Can it be done another way?

To his credit, Edward did recognise that semaphore positions could be reduced to numerical equivalents and that only 32 combinations were required to represent the alphabet and numerals. He also recognised that he only needed five beams of light to generate these 32 combinations, rather than 16 beams to represent 2 semaphore arms and 8 clock positions.

Some years later, after the invention of Morse code, Edward did re-examine his method of using five beams instead of one beam, but he concluded that a flashing single beam required too much concentration by the operator, as opposed to the simplicity of his five steady beams.

At this point Edward's notebook adopts a somewhat jubilant tone, probably because he believed that he had cracked the task of defining the problem at hand. He was not to know then that his problems were only just beginning. Edward adds that he discussed his findings with Elsie, the housekeeper.

In view of his personal views about women and social equality, it is most likely that Edward treated his housekeeper more like a house-guest than a domestic servant. Indeed, the word 'keeper' is crossed out and replaced with 'guest'. They certainly had meals together, because his notebook often refers to their discussions over dinner.

Sunday, 19 May 1816
Discussed semaphore problems with Elsie – the house guest.
Excellent cook and companion. More attractive and wholesome
than I considered at first sight. Flawless skin and smells fresh.
Delightful. Explained nature of problem. Listens well and
prompts me to ask myself questions that reveal surprising
answers. Isolate light from everything incl. weather. Why not a
cable of very thin glass rods. V. flexible. Must test theory
immediate.
EUREKA.

In this case, the notebook is marginally more detailed about Miss Hopkins, but still terse and cryptic. Essentially, after dinner that evening he sat chatting to Elsie, and little by little began to greatly appreciate her company. He began to see her in a different light. She was not well educated and at first sight was quite plain. It wasn't her mouth or her eyes or her hair, but rather the whole put together that he found attractive. She certainly had a flawless complexion that needed no artificial enhancements, and she always smelt fresh and clean, which in his eyes equated with good personal hygiene. He had never looked at her this way before, but now that he had, he was surprised at how well he perceived her.

Piecing together the brief notebook comments, it seems that during their conversation he mentioned that he had a serious decision to make. He wasn't expecting her to understand the technical details, but she listened in silence as he explained his dilemma. To his surprise, she grasped his situation immediately and made a series of comments and observations, which prompted him to clarify these points in his own mind. Gradually, with her interaction, the answer emerged from the clouds in his mind. He had to isolate the beams of light from the weather. He could put them inside tunnels under the ground, or perhaps pipes or tubes of metal, or even tubes of glass. Why tubes of glass if the beams could be carried by rods of glass? If so, then why not filaments of glass? Perhaps even hair fine filaments. Perhaps five filaments could be made into a cable and hung on posts above ground. The notebook comments end with the word EUREKA.

Monday, 20 May 1816
Glass blowers made several thin rods of diff diam. Measured flexibility and visibility. Best option 1/32- inch rod, easily visible to naked eye – bend radius 18-inch. V. Astonished that problem is solved, thanks to Elsie. Rod diam not accurate. Difficult to make so thin and uniform. Smaller diam, hair fine rods are more easily bent but more difficult to see. Microscopes not telescopes. 1/32 is most practical.

The following day, Edward embarked on a lengthy series of experiments, passing light beams through glass rods and tubes of various diameters. The notebook lists the results and the bend radius of each tube or rod. Based on these results, Edward selected the best compromise, i.e. the largest diameter (to avoid using microscopes) and the smallest bend radius (to make cable laying easier). He concluded that 1/32-inch diameter was easily visible with the naked eye and could be wound onto spools of 36 inches diameter with no risk of fractures. Edward can be forgiven for avoiding hair fine filaments, because he lived in an age where big and robust were beautiful. The world was not yet ready for micro-engineering.

GLASS CABLES

Edward even comments in his notebook that he is astounded at the direction his mind has taken. Nothing could have been further from his original thoughts. He generously gives the credit to Elsie for guiding him towards a glass filament.

Tuesday 4 June 1816
Much more testing with rods in liquids, bent and straight. No proper method to measure brightness. Crown glass and flint glass work best. Soda glass not so good. Immersed in water works well but not practical. Tried shellac in alcohol – just as good even when dry. Most practical method. Cannot understand why coating glass improves brightness. Does it make the glass a mirror?

We don't know whether Edward was familiar with the concept of total internal refraction, but his notebook describes a series of experiments with straight glass rods and tubes illuminated by a candle, and then a series of tests with bent rods and tubes immersed in various liquids including water. His conclusion was that a beam of light could be conducted through a glass rod or tube, even around severe bends, and that the brightness of the beam could be improved by surrounding the rod with certain liquids. His notes make no mention of the difference in refractive index between the glass and the liquid. However, he did comment that some types of glass appear to work better than others; for example, flint and crown glass appear to work best (higher refractive index).

Surrounding the glass filaments with a liquid was obviously going to be a problem, but the notebook does not mention any reference to a solution of shellac in alcohol. Most likely, Edward probably tried this solution, which would have worked, simply because it was readily available from the cabinet makers in the workshop. Probably, the shellac solution dried out naturally, and even that worked too.

Edward's workshop did not have its own glass furnace: they reheated glass rods and tubes made by Whitefriars Glass Works, near the Temple, just down the road. Indeed, two of his best glass blowers previously worked at Whitefriars, and it was these two who suggested Shola pith as a protective packing material for the five filaments, because that is what Whitefriars used when shipping delicate glass objects. The notebook records that Edward went to Whitefriars to see what Shola pith looked like and where to purchase some. On the spur of the moment, he ordered several sacks.

Friday, 7 June 1816
Visit to Whitefriars to see shola pith. Strange material – like cork but more resilient. Glass workers demonstrated light passing through bent rods. Lead glass is best for this. Impressed by knowledge and skill. Showed me how rods were made.

Pulling a molten drop of glass at right rate in smooth motion. Highly skilled. An education.

Clearly it was time to visit the fountain of knowledge, so Edward took time off to walk down to the glassworks near the Temple and to introduced himself. His notebook reveals that he was most surprised to find that the glass workers were already familiar with the ability of glass rods and tubes to conduct light round bends. They witnessed the effect daily. They even took the time to heat up a nearby glass rod in a gas flame assisted by foot bellows to produce a 'blue' flame, which they explained was much hotter than the normal sooty yellow flame used for illumination. Although only the centre of the length of rod was heated, the end tip glowed orange but wasn't hot at all. They even bent the rod to demonstrate that light could be conducted around bends. It was they who told him that lead glass was the best to use.

Edward was even entertained to a demonstration of how hand-made rod was produced, and that three-foot lengths were preferred because that was an arm's length. It seems that the diameter was determined by the 'sweep' rate (i.e. the rate at which the glass glob was drawn from the furnace) and that the diameter was kept constant by the rhythm of the 'sweep'. In other words, making the rods was a highly skilled operation. Again, it was these workers who told him that quarter inch rod was the easiest to make in one-yard lengths

43

and maintain a constant diameter. Finer rods could be produced but it was exceptionally difficult to preserve a constant diameter and maintain straightness, and the wastage rate was much higher. His notebook has a comment that the visit was 'an education'.

Tuesday 11 June 1816

Ordered shola pith. Tried to imagine two-way cable with 10 glass rods encased in shola bound with cotton and bitumen.

Diam of one rod=1/32 inch

Length=5280 feet

Density=162 lbs/cu.ft

Weight of one rod=18.2 lbs per mile

Shola core diam =0.5 inch

Shola length= 5280 feet

Shola density=8 lbs/cu.ft

Shola weight=230 lbs/mile

Waxed Cotton helix (1 inch wide)

Cotton binding weight=25.7 lbs/ mile.

Ignore shellac

Assume bitumen coating is 0.02 inches

Assume density is 62 lbs/cu.ft

Weight of bitumen coating=3 lbs/mile

Weight 10 rods=182

 shola 230

cotton 25

bitumen=3

TOTAL=440 lbs/mile

2-mile cable=880 lbs.

The next entry in the notebook concerns Edward's attempt to calculate the weight of a one-mile length of cable containing 10 filaments encased in Shola pith, i.e. a two-way compound cable, bound with cotton tape and waterproofed with bitumen. According to these calculations a mile of cable would weigh 440 lbs. If the cable was wound onto a wooden spool, it could be rolled onto and off a cart by two men, possibly using a wooden ramp. He was satisfied that such an arrangement would not present any transportation difficulties.

In view of his recent experience at the glassworks, Edward decided to involve his own metal workers in the design of a means to connect these one-mile lengths into a continuous cable, perhaps long enough to stretch from London to Portsmouth (about 72 miles). His only stipulation was that the connection had to be a single simple device that ensured that all ten filaments were accurately aligned.

Edward then spent some hours discussing the problem of cutting the ends of the glass filaments and joining them to the next cable length of filaments. The solution had to be a practical proposition that could be carried out in remote locations in the depths of the countryside. It was crucial that the joint should be near perfect in terms of transmitting light across the joint. Although Edward had a long-proven record of being the 'ace' problem solver, in this instance he was delegating the task to his craftsmen. No doubt his visit to Whitefriars had influenced this approach.

Friday 14 June 1816
Metal workers made precision brass fittings for all ten filaments. Perhaps use it to hold glass for grinding. Only one way to connect – offset screw. Masterpiece.

With surprising alacrity, the metal workers, presented Edward with their solution in the form of an exquisitely machined brass couplings in male and female versions, about one inch in diameter. They had even spoken to the lens grinders about using the coupling as a holder for grinding and polishing the tips of the filaments flat for the best possible joint. The couplings also had a cunning feature, (an off-set screw) to secure the two parts together to ensure perfect alignment. Altogether it was a masterpiece, which was confirmed in his notebook.

The glass workers also confirmed that grinding and polishing the filament ends was the only way to ensure near perfect transmission, but even optically flat ends may not mate perfectly, and that some sort of fluid interface might be necessary. Water would be perfect because of its low refractive index, but the film of water would soon dry out, so it had to be a fluid with a low evaporation rate such as an oil of some sort. The notebook has the comment 'Neats Foot' (a low viscosity oil, with low evaporation and good tolerance to low temperatures). Evaporation was not really a problem because the brass coupling could be made virtually air-tight.

As always, Edward adopted a very practical outlook on the whole process. No matter how many or how few joints were used, each one is bound to diminish the intensity of the original beam of light. Similarly, the length of glass filament will do the same. His next task was to determine a practical and acceptable compromise, which could only be done by making a real cable with real couplings and measuring the overall deterioration in the brightness of the transmitted beam. Provided the beam of light could be detected by the human eye, then that was the acid test. To set this process in motion he would have to get approval from the partners upstairs.

Thursday 20 June 1816
(S) suggests making test cable without A & C approval. Must be done to test loss of brightness through cable and couplings. Brass couplings ordered from B/ham.

Sybil came to Edward's rescue according to the notebook. Essentially, she advised him that provided experimental work had a strong potential for future profitable business, then it was up to Edward's judgement. Only if the level of investment was great, then he would need approval from upstairs. The two dozen tiny brass castings were well within his authority. Creating the equipment and the process for making glass filaments by the mile was a decision for upstairs. There was no need for Edward to reveal his hand just yet. Edward promptly ordered the castings from a firm in Birmingham. His own metal workers would do the final machining in the workshop because it required great accuracy.

So far, Edward had not spoken to the partners upstairs about his plans for an optical telegraph. There was much to do yet before he had a comprehensive plan to put forward for their approval and much depended on how the Admiralty would respond. In the meantime, he spent an afternoon contemplating how operators would send and receive code signals or characters transmitted as beams of light. He set out several cut pieces of pasteboard on his desk, weighted with coins. A silver six-penny piece (known as a tanner) represented an illuminated filament and a copper penny piece represented a key or button, of the locking type that would stay in position once depressed and which could be released separately. He started with five cards with silver coins on, but soon realised that he would need a sixth card and coin, for which he used a shilling (known as a bob) as a weight.

Friday 21 June1816
Damnation. Just tested procedure for sending messages. Need extra link between receiver and sender to signal ready. Cable now 12 filaments. V. angry with stupid self. Felt better after

dinner with (E). Much merriment about couplings (M & F). Later engaged in coupling. V pleasing for both.

The reason for this was because he realised that the receiving operator would need to tell the sending operator that she was ready to receive. While the sending operator was waiting for the ready signal, she could be pressing the buttons or keys for the next code. As soon as the sender received the ready signal she could press the 'send' button, which exposed the filaments attached to the depressed keys to the light source, which in turn illuminated the filament ends in front of the receiver. The receiver now becomes a sender and repeats the process to the next station in the line. There was nothing complicated about the procedure: it was simply a case of duplicating the illuminated filaments by depressing the corresponding buttons.

For some inexplicable reason he felt angry and annoyed that he would require an extra filament for the 'ready' signal. His bad mood followed him all the way home, but by the end of a sumptuous dinner prepared and served by Elsie, his mood had softened a little. Elsie was anxious to hear about how Edward's plans were progressing, and so Edward explained about the method of making cable joints and why the couplings were called male and female. This caused great merriment between them both, and with the laughter came relief from his mood. A series of very cryptic abbreviations

49

follow in the notebook, suggesting that Edward and Elsie also engaged in coupling during the night.

Saturday, 21 June 1816
Feeling v. bright. Must accept 12 filaments. New cable weight 476 lbs/mile. Real test essential. Theory not enough. 2-mile cable=952 lbs (half ton). Good weight for transport by horse & cart.

The following day, Edward describes himself as exceptionally bright and amenable, and fully accepts the necessity for a sixth filament. As if for confirmation he re-calculates the weight of a mile length of cable with two groups of six filaments as 476 lbs. To make matters clear, he describes the one- mile length as 'nominal', because he needs to manufacture a dozen or so couplings, to test how many of them can be connected back to back and still transmit enough light to be detectable with the naked eye. In effect this crucial test would determine how many lengths of cable can be connected together before a repeater station is required. A repeater station is simply a human person who repeats the code or message using a fresh source of light. Edward notes that if the source is sunlight, then no repeater stations would be needed. If the source is an Argand lamp then Edward is hopeful that he can run for ten miles between each repeater station, i.e. ten pairs of couplings with a one-mile cable between each coupling, or a two-mile cable with only five pairs of couplings, but he knows he must test this theory.

Edward's major obstacle was the absence of a reliable repeater device equivalent to the electric relay, which would have allowed him to dispense with all his repeater stations. This obstacle remained until late in the 19th century, when it was discovered that the resistance of selenium was dependent on the ambient light. Selenium itself was discovered at about the same time as Edward was developing his optical cable, much earlier in the 19th century.

THE MASTER PLAN

Wednesday, 26 June 1816
Possible future of Optical cable. Ignore public – too unreliable and unpredictable. Too expensive to cover whole nation. Needs huge finance. Last option is Admiralty, but bad payers. Not enough profit in cable, but good profits in expensive sending/receiving cypher machines. V expensive and complex. Repeater machines v. simple but look expensive. Good selling points – day and night operation – not affected by weather. Cyphers needed – substitution codes too easy to break. Possible to use extra letters (FOG)and change the order (SCRAMBLE). Don't like it, but Navy or nothing.

The Notebook has a very brief but revealing note about the extent of Edward's plans for the optical telegraph. In the first instance, Edward is not convinced that an optical telegraph would capture the public's imagination or would become a commercial success. He recognised that to cover the entire country would require enormous capital investment, far beyond the means of the partners upstairs and all their many friends and business associates. His only option was to form an alliance with the Admiralty to get his project up and running. In this scenario, the number of stations is limited, and the cable distances are modest. Edward is convinced that day and night operation at half the cost was sufficient bait to capture the support of the

Admiralty. Hopefully his optical telegraph would work so well while the Navy waits for its semaphore system to become operational, that they may never bother to finish it. Edward indicates that he doesn't expect his telegraph cable to make a fortune from the Navy: it is merely a means to an end.

What Edward is really after is a Navy contract to supply cypher machines, i.e. machines that can convert English text into codes that are virtually impossible to break. Obviously, these same machines can work backwards to convert codes into plain English text. In this context, his optical telegraph would transmit all messages in cypher in order to maintain the utmost secrecy, whether they need it or not. This is the long-term strategy that Edward wants the Admiralty to buy into. His reasoning was probably based on the fact, that manufacturing the optical cable and installing it would probably be a singular, and inexpensive event, despite the lengths involved. The cypher machines, on the other, hand were complex intricate devices that would look and be expensive. Most importantly, his company would have exclusive rights to manufacture them, at least initially.

The simplest way of keeping visual signals a secret, when anybody can observe them, as is the case with semaphore, is to use a private code that renders the message incomprehensible to anybody who is not in possession of the codebook. To do this reliably requires a machine that generates codes automatically, as well as de-cyphering code back into a human readable form. Humans can make mistakes, whereas machines don't.

Although the notebook does not refer to specific methods of breaking cyphers, it does mention that Edward made some attempts to use letter frequency to decode a simple message. Edward concludes that simple letter substitution was dangerously too easy to break. He had worked out that it must be possible to measure the frequency or number of times a certain letter occurs in any language. If he had a table of these frequencies, then it would be a simple matter to decode any message involving a simple substitution cypher.

The notebook continues by speculating about methods of making cyphers more complex. Edward gives an example of how extra letters could be added at the end of a message to artificially alter the normal letter frequency, which he describes as 'fog'. These extra letters occur after the end-of-message signal, so that they would be discarded by the cypher machine. He also refers to a method of changing the order of the letters in the original message according to a simple mathematical rule, and then re-assembling the message prior to using a cypher, which he calls 'scrambling'. Edward remarks that when the letters are re-ordered, the message is so totally confusing that it hardly needs the final cypher. Edward writes that he is confident that he can make a machine that performs these functions.

He wasn't completely happy about depending on the Admiralty for funding because they had a bad reputation for blowing hot and cold, depending on whether Great Britain was at war or not. What he needed was a commercial connection that would benefit from rapid communications, such as shipping insurance, newspapers and certain government departments. Railways had barely started but if they expanded across the country then these too could be potential customers. He was uncertain how the public in general would react to rapid communications. If it was cheap enough he could be overwhelmed by over-use. It was an incalculable conundrum: there were too many uncontrollable variables. Besides, funding a nation wide optical cable would be prohibitive. Edward concludes that it was the Navy or nothing.

Tuesday, 2 July 1816
How many operators? Perhaps 2 – one up and one down. No skill. Simple to train. Just copying illuminated filaments. Monkeys could do it. Argand lamps need filling. Live in staff? Could be expensive. Round the clock working also expensive and weekends. Admiralty decision. Could we use coal gas flames?

The next entry in the notebook refers to Edward's speculations about the number of female telegraphists he might need at each station. Initially he proposes just two telegraphists, who between them would handle down-line and up-line messages. No skill was required because the operators because they only need to duplicate the incoming illuminated filaments, and periodically refill the Argand lamps to maintain the source illumination.

Edward even speculates that he could use coal gas flames provided by compressed gas in containers, although this would present him with a difficult problem of ensuring a continuous supply. For those areas that already produce coal gas, this would obviously not be a problem. Ideally, they should be live-in staff to ensure daily attendance particularly in remote locations. The alternative is to make sure that the cable routes run close to villages and towns. Edward admits that he has no immediate answer to weekend working, or for providing food and water for the operators, but was prepared to leave those problems for a later date.

Tuesday, 9 July 1816
Shola arrived. V strange stuff like cork but lighter. Cut into short granules (kibbler) and stick together with weak gum. Pressure cast into sticks with grooves. Metal boys to make mould. Spent all day trying different gums. Resin in turpentine is best. Grooves in shola grips glass well, Lubrication? Keep waste to make shola paper sheets. Thank goodness for my set of bench posts. (E) says cable is work of genius.

The next entry in the notebook records the delivery of the sacks of Shola pith. Edward remarks that it is a very strange material, like dried twigs from a bush or shrub, except that it is exceedingly light-weight, very pliable and compressible like cork. Indeed, the sacks were labelled Indian Cork. The material was so much like real cork, that it occurred to him that perhaps he could use real cork, although cork was much heavier. In its present form, the material was of no practical use because he needed a continuous length about a half-inch in diameter, or preferably sticks about two to three feet in length that could be joined end to end to form a continuous core for the filaments.

His first thought was to cut up the twigs into granules of 1/16th inch diameter, and then to mix these particles with a paste or glue and compress the mix into a half-inch rod inside a mould of some sort. Finally, the rod would need to be dried in an oven. Edward notes that the glue is only needed to stick the particles together and not to bond the whole stick into a solid mass. He needed to maintain the pliability and compressibility, because it was these two features that would protect the fragile glass filaments. He also observed that the filaments would probably need some form of lubrication to assist with bending all twelve filaments inside the finished cable.

There is a strange reference to 'bench posts', which I assume were similar to current 'retort stands and clamps', which are often used as a temporary means to hold laboratory equipment in place for test purposes. I would guess that the 'bench posts' were similar devices that Edward had probably made during his apprenticeship at Cummings. These would have enabled Edward to construct a rigid framework to clamp clockwork engine to, as well as other bits of equipment, just to test out an idea or concept.

The metal workers provided Edward with a half-inch brass pipe and a turned iron rod inside. Edward had already decided to use tree resin dissolved in turpentine, because he didn't want to disturb the thin layer of shellac on the glass filament (shellac is not soluble in turpentine). It must have taken Edward some time to fill the brass tube with the porridge-like mixture of Shola pith and various concentrations of resin in turpentine, and to cast half-inch sticks of Shola. Edward reports that he spent most of a day making and drying Shola sticks, before he found the right combination of resin concentration and the compression pressure to preserve the important properties of Shola. This was yet another component of the cable making process that would never become a Patent, just an industrial secret.

As always, Edward was a practical man, and immediately set about designing a machine to granulate the Shola pith, which he called a 'kibbler'. The next item on the drawing board was a press to form the Shola paste into 24-inch long sticks, based on his very simple piston press that worked so well in his experiments. The only difference was a die in the end of the brass tube to form the twelve grooves around the circumference for the glass filaments to nestle into. Basically, Edward had constructed a crude piston extruder.

At about this time Karl Drais invented a hand cranked meat grinder (mincing machine), which would have been perfect for extruding the Shola core. Although this meat grinder was popular in Germany, the technology didn't reach England for many years.

Nevertheless, Edward's device worked well enough to produce several batches of dried sticks with longitudinal grooves. To Edward's delight, hand-made filaments could be pressed into the grooves tightly enough to hold several sticks together end-to-end. He reports his impatience to take a stick home, complete with waxed cotton tape binding, to show Elsie. For her part, Elsie was hugely impressed with the cable and its complexity, and promptly declared Edward to be a genius. Edward makes no comment about the accolade.

Tuesday, 16 July 1816
Glassmen v good but making constant diam rod at 1/32 inch exceeding difficult. Observed glassmen. Seems problem is the continuous feed of ¼ inch rod. Timed how long to heat rods and join. Metal workers made brass nip rolls. Should work. Also made worm drive to feed rods at constant speed, driven by air engine not steam. Too dangerous. Joined ¼ rods at speed 3 feet/min. All cheered first run.

Added brass nip rolls to bench post frame to remove bulge at rod joint. Hot rods supported on pear wood grooved rollers. Looks good.

While Edward obviously had every faith in his glass workers, he does comment that the hand-made filaments were variable in diameter and that there was considerable wastage from cutting out the small sections that were not on size. Edward had carefully observed the two glass craftsmen at work and with their help he sketched a device for fusing quarter inch rods end-to-end using a fish tail gas burner assisted with compressed air to produce a hot blue flame. With his pocket watch he timed how long it took for the glass rod ends to glow orange so that they fused on contact.

The metal workers turned two grooved brass nip rollers to roll out any uneven bulges and to partially cool the joint. The two rods were supported on a row of pear wood grooved rollers to maintain alignment. These rollers were turned by the cabinet- makers. It soon emerged that the secret behind the fusing process was to keep the speed of the two glass rods constant. The whole workshop was now involved with impatient enthusiasm. Despite this, it took the metalworkers the rest of the day to make a worm wheel drive and a tiny piston engine driven by compressed air, to power the wood and brass rollers. Edward insisted on compressed air because he needed to control the speed accurately with a needle valve. A large variation in the worm rotation was much less in the wheel rotation.

Everybody in the workshop gathered around to witness the small device working under power. Indeed, they all cheered when the first successful joint emerged. The initial speed was quite slow but improved considerably when they attached two more fishtail burners to heat the moving glass rod more quickly. At 3 feet per minute Edward knew that this tiny device could produce over two miles of filament per day when drawn out.

Wednesday, 17 July 1816
Observed how glassmen draw out fine threads. Again, secret is to draw out at constant speed. This time use a pear wood drum to wind up filament rotating at 7.6 rpm. Filament ran thin so added more heaters. Triumph. Correct size filament by the mile. Drum speed critical to filament diameter. Needs constant watching. Made test samples. Showed (E) at home. Amazed.

The next stage was again carried out with the help of the glass craftsmen who assisted Edward to simulate the drawing out process. Once again, a fishtail burner heated up the leading tip of the rod emerging from the joining machine to maintain a glowing tip which was then drawn out by hand as a hair fine thread and attached to a pear wood drum revolving at eight times the speed of the glass rods (about 7.6 r.p.m.). It was immediately obvious that more heat was required at the rod end to melt more glass. The thread was too fine because there was insufficient melted glass. A second burner cured the problem, and within minutes the device was producing a continuous stream of 1/32 inch glass filament.

For Edward this was a moment of triumph. The collective efforts of the workmen and his own ideas had resulted in a process for producing filaments of glass to order. Obviously, the shellac solution in alcohol needed to be applied and dried before the winding drum, but otherwise Edward knew that he would be able to make accurately sized filaments by the mile. The length that they had already made could be used to test out the filament joint making process, and a back-to-back multi-joint test would reveal the answer to how many joints they could tolerate. Edward cut a short length from the drum to take home to show Elsie.

Thursday, 18 July 1816
Changed drum drive – too coarse. Used 3-roll grooved worm drive for better control. Added dancing brake roller to drum drive with friction brake. Drum over speeds and applies brake to match 3-roll speed. Added metal clip to drum to grab filament end. Avoids stopping process to start new drum. Fitted magnifier to 3-roll drive to observe exit filament diam. Getting better all the time.

The following day, Edward improved the filament drive arrangement with a set of three grooved pear wood rollers with the centre roll offset to maintain the tension at constant speed. The previous drive drum was modified with a friction bearing and a brake roller. The friction bearing was just a plain brass on iron bearing packed with hard grease, which basically idled if the brake was applied. The drum speed was increased slightly so that any over-speed caused the brake roller to lift, which in turn applied the brake and effectively disengaged the drum drive. The drum itself was modified with a small metal clamp to grip the free end of the glass filament during the start-up stage.

The operators could now manually start the process off by holding back the drum by hand until they could thrust the leading end of the filament into the metal clamp. Meanwhile the glass workers fitted a large magnifying glass and scale to the discharge end of the three-roll drive so that they could continuously observe how thick the filament was by slowing down or speeding up the little engine that powered the three-roll tension drive.

Up to this point, the workers had conspired with Edward to conceal the various components of the machine around the workshop, so as not to attract any attention during the daily morning inspections. However, in its current state, the machine ran the whole length of the workshop and could no longer be hidden. It was time for Edward to reveal his plan to the partners, armed with a short length of fully assembled cable.

Friday, 19 July 1816
Usually filament process hidden away. Time to tell A & C
about successful process and plans for optical cable. Told them
real profits were in cypher machines not cable. Good response. V
supportive. Warned that cypher machines would be top secret.
Patents unlikely.

In the company of the two partners, Edward proudly announced that the firm now had a unique process for making optical telegraph cable in sufficient quantities to cover the whole country, and moreover it had not cost the firm any money. It was the last comment that produced the smiles, and the two partners were keen to examine the sample that Edward produced. Edward went on to explain his plans for involving the Admiralty, particularly with respect to his thoughts on making cypher machines that produced unbreakable codes. He got the immediate impression that, for the partners, codes and cypher machines were foreign territory and that his simple explanations were falling on deaf ears.

He did warn them that the optical cable itself may not be a huge source of revenue, unless the public clamour for it, and even then, it would require astronomic investment before it could make any real money. The cypher machines were altogether different; they were high quality complex instruments and would almost certainly be classified as top secret: so secret that it was unlikely that they would be permitted to Patent the devices. It would not surprise Edward if the Navy decided to put a guard on the premises day and night to preserve the secret nature of these machines. It was time to seek the partner's permission to follow up his ideas with the Admiralty, which they gave without reservation.

Edward must have spent some considerable time working on the concept of cypher machines because there are several short reminder notes before he launches into a full description of the device.

Monday, 22 July 1816
Jacquard: paper tapes better than wooded plates with holes.
Letterpress type for receiving station.
Clockwork engine.
Automatic rewind?
Light source boosted at repeater stations.
Engraved circular disc to compose messages.
Returns to zero after each letter selected.
Steel needle disc to punch the paper tape. Moves as composing disc is moved.
Perhaps ratchet to change code with each selection.
Paper is punched when operator presses key.
Punch disc has 42 sets of needles (extra 10 for numerals)
Message header numerals are always un-coded.

In 1801 Joseph Marie Jacquard invented a power loom that could produce weave patterns based on holes punched in wooden plates. Clearly, Edward knew of this loom, but he doesn't say if he ever saw one. He is not attracted to the idea of holes in wooden plates, but he is very much in favour of punching holes in a roll of paper tape, both for creating a coded message and for de-coding a message.

His sending and receiving stations all used buttons or keys, which could easily be adapted to punch holes in paper tape. Similarly, the paper tape could easily activate letter-press typeface at the receiving end or could activate the exposure of the light source to the glass filaments at the sending end. Paper tape was a cheap, simple, and flexible medium that could produce readable results, which could also be indexed, character-by-character, with a simple clockwork engine. If he was extremely cunning, he could even design the buttons or keys to rewind the clockwork spring.

According to the notebook, Edward visualised that at the sending station there would be a circular brass disc (note the 19th century spelling of disc: computers had not yet been invented) engraved with letters of the alphabet and numerals, with a target pointer. The disc is rotated by hand to align the desired letter with the pointer. Beneath the brass disc is another metal disc containing 42 sets of steel needles, each set consisting of various combinations of five needles. The two discs can be rotated simultaneously by means of a milled knob. With the desired letter at the pointer position, a key is pressed, which punches the corresponding set of needles through the paper tape located immediately below the needles. When the key is released, it retracts the needles and it indexes the paper tape forwards by one character (approx. quarter inch). To change the code, only the steel needle disc needs to be changed. A three-digit signature would allow for 999 different code discs.

Edward also notes the possibility of adding a ratchet mechanism to the steel disc so that it moves one position relative to the brass disc every time a letter is selected. In effect the code is changed for every letter. This would defeat any attempt at decoding messages using letter frequency tables.

Edward notes that for maximum security, the original paper tape would be generated by the sender in person. The tape would then be given to a telegraph operator, who will have no idea of the original message because the tape is in code form. This level of security applies throughout the optical telegraph system and its repeater stations until it reaches its destination. The destination receiving station would generate a paper tape which would be handed to the recipient in person. The recipient takes the paper tape to their own personal de-coding machine, which is effectively a sending machine, but working backwards to produce a printed-paper message tape. Each steel needle disc is numbered, and this number is transmitted at the start of any message, so that the recipient knows which de-coding disc to use. The only two people who witness the message are the original author and the intended recipient.

Tuesday, 23 July 1816
Paper tape reader.
Set of five blunt needles search for holes in paper tape.
If needle penetrates then cam is activated.
Five sets of cams with teeth. 1,2,8,16.
Extra cam with 11 teeth for numerals
Message header numerals are always un-coded.

Edward then writes more specifically about the way that the paper tape reader device works. Outwardly, the personal coding and de-coding devices look the same. They both have a paper tape spool, they both have a brass disc with letters and numbers engraved on the face. They both have a target pointer, and both are driven by clockwork engines, which are wound by a crank handle at the side.

The major difference is in the steel disc below the brass face. In the coding machine the steel disc has sets of five needles underneath each letter, whereas the de-coding machine has letter-press typeface beneath. The de-coding machine also has a tape reading attachment that essentially pushes blunt pins through the punched holes in the tape. Whatever the combination of punched holes, then the corresponding pins will penetrate the tape and engage a series of toothed cams. The first pin activates a one-tooth cam, the second activates a two-tooth cam, the third activates a four-tooth cam, the fourth activates an eight-tooth cam, and finally the fifth activates a 16-tooth cam. The five cams are staggered around the drive shaft so that they present a total of 31 teeth driving the gearwheel linked to the brass disc. Only the activated cams can rotate when driven by the clockwork engine. This rotation causes the brass and metal discs to rotate a specific number of positions based on the cam tooth count. When the cam shaft stops rotating, the clockwork motor stamps the corresponding typeface onto the paper tape. The ink is then refreshed, and the paper tape is indexed forwards one position. Simultaneously the two discs are rotated back to their start positions by an internal coil spring. This process is repeated until the end of the tape. The recipient is only required to load the paper tape correctly, and check that the code number corresponds with the original paper tape: the rest is automatic, apart from rewinding the clockwork engine.

Originally, Edward intended the paper tape to be half inch wide but changed this to inch wide tape so that he could print onto the same tape as the punched holes, which simplified the whole printed tape mechanism. He also wanted to pre-punch a line of small holes down the centre line of the tape because he wanted to use a more positive drive for the tape with a pin-wheel, that engaged with the centre holes. He rather liked the idea of having a permanent record of the original coded message as well as the de-coded message. As an added extra, he included a pawl that rested on the main spring of the clockwork engine, which popped up a wooden peg to indicate when the main spring needed re-winding.

Friday, 16 August 1816
Wider tape required (1-inch)
Ink application poor. Smudges easily. Not good enough. Made cotton tape soaked in ink — beeswax, linseed, lampblack, turpentine. Dried in oven. Works very well but could dry out. Keep in waxed paper bag.

Initially the inking system didn't work as well as he had hoped, and it took Edward some time to come up with an improved method, using a reel of cotton tape coated on one side with an ink mixture based on beeswax, turpentine, linseed oil and lampblack. This tape had to be oven dried before winding it onto a wooden reel. The same mechanism that indexed the punched paper tape also indexed the ink ribbon.

In 1808, Italian Pellegrino Turri invented a typewriter. He also invented carbon paper to provide the ink for his machine. Sadly, this information was not available to Edward at that time, so he had to invent his version of a typewriter ribbon from scratch. He did at least remember to package each wooden bobbin and its ribbon inside a waxed paper bag so that it wouldn't dry out completely during storage.

Tuesday, 20 August 1816
Damnation again. Forgot the numeric key. Header numbers are un-coded. Need an extra cam with 11 teeth. 42 segments mean

70

steel disk is 7-inch diameter. Engraved brass – expensive. Perhaps ceramic or glass labels.

Fortunately, Edward spotted a flaw in his initial design: The receiver had no means of identifying which code disc to use. He had to incorporate a signature at the start of the message to inform the recipient which code disc to use. Edward reports that it took him almost a whole day to come up with a solution, because he had also forgotten to account for the 'numeric' key (open bracket), which switched on numerals as opposed to letters. The close bracket key switched off numerals back to letters. His solution involved adding an extra first cam, with eleven teeth, to select letterpress dies for letters, whereas the single tooth cam was engaged only when the open bracket key was depressed, and only disengaged when the close bracket key was depressed. This also meant that the upper brass disc and the lower steel disc had to be divided into 42 segments. At half-inch segment pitch, the discs would have to be about 7-inches in diameter. At first, he intended to engrave the brass disc, but eventually decided to use round ceramic (or glass) inserts, because they would be easier to read. The bracket keys determined which of the two first cams were active or not i.e. letters or numbers. The next decision he made was that the machines would have keys for the two bracket symbols, and the numerals (0-9) were in the same place (the first ten disc segments), so that it didn't matter which disc was currently in the decoder, the first header containing the correct disc number, as the first three digits, would always be printed correctly. This would allow the decoder operator to change discs appropriately.

Monday, 26 August 1816
Instructed works to build 2 full scale coding and decoding machines, so we can fully test them. Prepare for Admiralty test. 2 new products – paper tape and ink ribbons.
Wednesday, 18 September 1816
Test machines completed. With (S) tested both with 100 characters. Excellent – coding less than 4 minutes. Decoder 90 seconds. Perfect. (S) astonished. Glassmen making polished couplings. Supply of ¼ rods on order with Whitefriars.

The workshop built two full-size working models of the coding and decoding machines according to Edward's detailed drawings, which allowed Sybil and himself to thoroughly test the devices before he presented them to the Admiralty for critical inspection. Edward and Sybil sat in his office, with Edward pretending to be a sender and Sybil pretended to be the receiver. He sent her 20 groups of five letters in less than three and a half minutes by his pocket watch.

They then sat back while the de-coding machine swallowed the paper tape and printed the entire message in one and a half minutes. Sybil was exceedingly impressed with the de-coder and sat transfixed during the de-coding process. She then checked each group of five letters, and finally announced a perfect match with the original. For

Edward, this was proof enough that his machines were ready for a demonstration. Sybil retired to her own office shaking her head and muttering how remarkable the whole process was.

Edward noted, with some satisfaction, that he had inadvertently created two new products; pre-punched rolls of paper tape, and letterpress ink ribbons. Everything helped.

The glass workers were given the task of preparing the brass couplings by inserting twelve filaments, sealed with shellac, and then grinding the tips flat, and finally polishing them. Apparently, they first tried grinding the tips one at a time, but this was very time consuming. Their final solution was to grind all twelve with a single large diameter disc as opposed to a small wheel. This improved the grinding rate enormously. The major obstacle was the length of the polishing cycle with jeweller's rouge. Edward's opinion was that perhaps a perfect finish was not required because he intended to use a liquid interface between the tip-to-tip joint. Perhaps he could just fire-polish the ends. Only the back-to-back test would confirm if he was right.

Wednesday, 25 September 1816
¼ rods arrived from Whitefriars. 700 rods per box. Enough for 1-mile cable and 2-mile cable. Day and night production

planned. Too important to go home. Stay day and night until done. (S) ordered food and drink supplies.

A week later, 3 boxes of quarter inch glass rods arrived from Whitefriars. Each box contained 700 rods in seven layers. A box would make a mile of filament, so he had enough to make one spool of one-mile and one spool of two-miles. It was Edward's plan to run the filament process continuously, day and night. This meant that the two glass craftsmen would have to work in rotation, just in case they had a breakage and needed to re-start the process. Jimmy and a young apprentice metalworker agreed to work a rota to keep the steam engine boiler going. Sybil organised the delivery of fresh bread, and a supply of cheese and ale from a nearby tavern. Edward himself, elected to remain in attendance for the whole run. He later added that this was a decision that he regretted.

It seems the first run started well and continued almost without mishap, until it started to get dark in the evening. Suddenly the glass-man watching the thickness gauge reported that the filament was thinning. He also noticed that the gas heater flame was lower than usual, so he opened the needle value to bring the flame back to normal. Edward reasoned that so many street lamps had been ignited that the local gas pressure had dropped.

Following the first mile, the filament was cut and then immediately thrust into the second winding drum. The glass-man on duty had been pre-warned about the gas supply and was standing-by ready for the increase at dawn. By the afternoon, a full two-mile filament had been completed, and the process was shut down. Edward admits that he was exhausted and retired to his office to take a nap.

Friday, 27 September 1816
Fell asleep. Exhausted. Home to (E). Slept badly.

Two hours later Sybil woke him with a cup of tea, just in time to lock up the workshop and go home. At least Edward now had sufficient filament to carry out meaningful tests. The weight of one-mile of single filament was just 4 lbs 8 oz and the weight of two-miles was 9 lbs. The weight of the wooden spool was about 40 lbs. The afternoon nap and speculation about the tests kept his brain active most of the night, so sleep only came in fitful bursts.

Edward assembled the workers to congratulate them on their efforts the previous week, in producing the one-mile spool and the two-mile spool. He told them that he was now ready to test which of the two spool sizes he intended to use. What he didn't tell them was that he knew of no method to measure the brightness of the light source at the termination of each spool.

Went to thank Whitefriars. While there picked up piece of green glass – looks black. Told glassmen to grind it to wedge shape to test loss of brightness in cable and couplings. Cabinet makers made nice box with Argand lamp and glass wedge. Also made nice box for my bench posts. Appreciate gift.

He took a break to clear his mind and took a stroll down to Whitefriars to thank them for the speedy supply of glass rods and to boast of his filament process. While he was at the glassworks he picked up a shapeless lump of what appeared to be black glass, which the workers assured him was a green 'drop-end' from the bottle blowing process. As soon as he got back to the workshop, he asked his glass-men to grind the lump of green glass into the shape of a cheese wedge. The thick end had to be kept thick enough to virtually prevent any light passing through. Obviously, the thin end would be almost transparent. The objective was to produce a piece of graded glass that would allow him to a compare the brightness of the filament termination against the brightness of the original Argand flame.

The cabinet-makers produced a testing box for Edward, which contained an Argand lamp and his green glass comparison scale, mounted vertically in a graduated slide. One side had a clamp for the cable coupling, which could be rotated, and the other side had a single comparison filament that could be viewed through the green glass scale. It was a simple matter to rate each filament in the cable by rotating the clamp, and to match the brightness by adjusting the green glass scale. The results were a surprise and a revelation.

The cabinet makers also gave Edward a gift of a box to hold all his bench posts and clamps. I assume that Edward normally kept these posts in a canvas bag or something similar. Perhaps the cabinet makers thought it was time that he had a proper box.

Friday 4 October 1816
Test results surprising.
Glass wedge not very accurate 3%. Dark room required.
1-mile cable loss 8%
2-mile cable loss 15%
1 coupling polished loss 6%
5 couplings polished loss 25%
1 coupling unpolished loss 8%
5 couplings unpolished loss 32%
Total loss 10-mile cable plus couplings 50%
Large loss but still easily visible.

Firstly, the comparison box was easy to use, but matching the brightness was much more difficult. Edward found that a darkened room helped. Even so, Edward suspected that the accuracy of the device was no better than plus or minus 3 percent. He quickly determined that the brightness loss in the one-mile cable was about 8 percent, and the loss in the two-mile cable was 15 percent. The brightness loss across one coupling was about 6 percent and across 5 couplings (back-to-back) was 25 percent. In effect this meant that the brightness loss down a ten-mile section of cable would be close to 45 percent, but this was still easily visible with the human eye. He also tested ground, but unpolished filament tips, which showed a loss of 8 percent for one coupling and 32 percent for five couplings. The total loss for a ten-mile unpolished cable was 50 percent but again still visible to the naked eye. Edward had every right to smile to himself: his concept worked.

Edward had designed both the sending and receiving machines to work at the rate of one character per second, but in his opinion, human operators would not be able to sustain this rate for any length of time. In his view humans would be lucky to achieve 2 to 3 seconds per character in a normal working day.

Tuesday, 8 October 1816
Cost of sending messages. Confirm ready=5 secs.
Average message 100 letters=25 words.
Send time station to station 8.5 minutes (5 mins).
Messages per 24-hr day 169 (288)
Operators 20/- per 8-hr day 60/- per 24-hr day
4d per 100 letters (2 and half d)
A penny per word would cover costs.
Premises rentals unknown. Perhaps semaphore stations.

The sending speed depends on the confirmation gap between any two stations. In the next note Edward calculates the capacity of the telegraph based on a conservative delay of 5 seconds between stations, i.e. 75 seconds delay between London and Portsmouth. He also allowed a similar delay between letters. For example, a 100-letter message (25 average words) would take 8 minutes 30 seconds to transmit, although he was quite certain that it could easily be done in 5 minutes. His telegraph could therefore handle between 169 and 288 messages of this size in any 24-hour period in both directions. Edward also calculates the running cost based on 20 shillings per 8-hour day per person. Each line uses three operators round the clock or 60 shillings per day, i.e. from 4 pence per 100-letter message to 2 1/2 pence (roughly a penny per word would cover his running costs). Renting premises was another matter, which all depended on whether he could use the new Admiralty telegraph stations.

Note the strange currency notation 20/-. The oblique stroke was used to separate the three units of currency; pounds, shillings and pence. This notation persisted for a further 156 years until 1972 when the British currency was decimalised. Fractions of a penny were used rather than decimal points.

Edward now turned his attention to comparing character-by-character messages and single characters, i.e. the codebook method. Privately he was convinced that character-by-character was the most flexible and the right direction to proceed. However, all the current semaphores used codebooks, as far as he was aware, possibly because they were so quick. Of course, his optical telegraph could be used to send codebook messages, but they were less secure at both ends of the line, because too many people had access to the message during the coding and de-coding stages. Codebook messages couldn't compete with his machines. He remembered Sybil's reaction to the de-coding machine and hoped that it would have the same effect on the Admiralty.

Monday 14 October 1816
Inserting filaments into shola core. Should be done in pairs on opposite sides. Shola very weak across core. Equal pressure from both sides. Insert with free running grooved wheels. Line speed ought to be 4 feet/min. Drying rate of bitumen probably slowest process. Estimated at 20 minutes- shorter if applied hot. Also melts wax on cotton layer. Instructed carpenters to build drying cabinet next to boiler room outside, 20 ft. long x 4 ft. high with pulley wheel to give double pass. Add talc dust after. Rotary fan inside to speed up drying. No naked flames – solvent very flammable.

The next item on Edward's optical telegraph agenda (not counting his normal everyday activities) was the combination and insertion of twelve glass filaments into the Shola pith core and spirally winding the cotton binding tape. Again, the throughput rate had to be at least one-mile of finished cable per day, and ten-miles per day would be even better. At a guess, Edward thought that the bitumen drying process would be the determining factor.

Rotary fans were known as far back as the Song dynasty in China, 800 years ago. More recently, John Desaguliers, a British engineer, demonstrated the successful use of a rotary fan system to draw out stagnant air from coal mines, in 1727, and later he installed a similar fan system in Parliament. Edward certainly knew about rotary fans, but was not aware of the design principles, but this did not deter him from using such a fan inside the drying chamber for the bitumen coating.

In view of the flammable nature of the solvents he decided against using hot air. Instead he depended on a high-volume fan to evaporate the solvents. It didn't matter how efficient the fan was: what mattered was whether it dried the bitumen coating quickly enough. In the notebook there is a sketch of a two-tier box about 20-feet long and four-feet high. At the far end a large diameter wooden pulley wheel (sheave) is shown. A threading up cord, to assist pulling through a new cable, is also shown. The coated cable would pass from the workshop, through this box alongside the boiler house, around the pulley, and back again into the workshop. At a speed of four-feet per minute the cable would have twenty minutes to dry.

As a quick test, Edward walked around the workshop for twenty minutes waving a two-foot length of cable, that he had coated by hand painting it. The surface was no longer tacky, but he couldn't tell what the bitumen was like below the surface. As a safeguard he decided to dust the cable with talc to prevent the cable sticking to itself. It was his opinion that applying a hot coating would assist the drying of the solvent. Edward notes that a hot water bath will be needed to heat the bitumen because there is too much risk of a fire from the flammable solvent if a naked flame was used for heating. We can see that Edward was exceedingly cautious, perhaps at times too cautious.

The final item that would complete the process was the device that inserted twelve filaments into the grooved Shola pith and bound it with cotton tape. Firstly, Edward sketched a frame containing two rows of six wooden spools mounted on iron axles so that they were free to rotate. All the filaments then pass over a cotton pad sitting in a dish of Neats Foot Oil to lubricate the glass filaments. The next component was the Shola loading station where the grooved sticks were manually aligned and pushed into the back end of the preceding stick, which was surrounded by twelve free-running wheels, which are mounted in line with the Shola grooves. These wheels were arranged in three groups of four wheels, so that the pressure is evenly distributed around the Shola stick. Each wheel consists of two brass discs which compress a cork disc between them.

It is this cork disc that presses the glass filaments into the grooves. This was then followed by two grooved brass nip rolls that grip the Shola stick and propel it forwards at the rate of four-feet per minute, directly into the device that spirally winds cotton tape around the cable. A small compressed air engine drives the nip rolls.

Friday, 18 October 1816
The shola stick with 12 glass inserts is pulled through a rotating spool of waxed cotton tape that covers the cable with helix of cotton tape. Friction brake on cotton spool too coarse. Causes comp. air engine to stall. Fixed counterbalance weight on spool arm. Much better. No need to warm wax cotton because hot bitumen does this.

The tape winder consisted of a heavy cast iron frame on legs with a hollow non-rotating shaft mounted on top, in line with the emerging unwrapped cable. At the end the iron shaft there was a brass gear wheel (free to rotate around the fixed shaft) driven by the same compressed air engine that drives the nip rolls. Attached to the brass gear wheel there was an iron bar, with a shaft for mounting the cotton tape bobbin. This arm rotates 12 times faster than the nip rolls, which produces a spiral of cotton tape wound at one-inch pitch. A friction brake on the bobbin allows the operator to adjust the tension in the cotton binding. The weight of the cotton tape bobbin at the end of the arm initially caused the air engine to stutter, so Edward

83

attached a counter balance weight to the brass gear wheel to smooth out the torque on the tiny air engine. Initially Edward intended to fit a small gas flame directed at another pair of nip rolls to heat the wax coating on the tape to bond it firmly, but Edward discarded this idea because this flame must be turned off if the cable flow stops at any time. Instead, Edward reasoned that the hot bitumen would provide enough heat to bond the wax on the cotton tape.

The bound cable was drawn through a bath of hot bitumen, and then any surplus was removed with brushes. At this point, during start-up, the leading end of the cable was gripped by a metal clamp attached to a cord that runs through the drying chamber, around the return wheel and back to the workshop. The cable was manually hauled through the drying chamber (only at start-up) and was then attached to a winding drum that maintained the tension. Prior to the winding drum there was a talc box that dusted the cable with talc. Any surplus was blown off with a jet of air. There are few details about the talc box in the notebook, so we must assume that Edward provided some means to avoid filling the workshop with talc dust.

Although the firm had a powerful steam engine driven by steam from the boiler house, cautious Edward was not happy about having a conventional mill shaft running down the workshop with countless leather drive belts all over the place. It was not so much the belt itself that was the problem; it was the joint in the belt that could grip hold of clothing or fingers or whatever to cause a serious accident. Edward much preferred to run iron pipes around the workshop, carrying compressed air, which he could tap into with flexible leather pipes. Edward was aware that condensation inside this pipe might be a problem, so he instructed Jimmy to routinely drain the stop-cocks. Of course, this meant he had to install a compressor, which the metal workers built themselves, as well as a reservoir tank, which again they made themselves. According to Edward, compressed air was relatively harmless, whereas scalding steam was an accident just waiting to happen.

Wednesday, 23 October 1816
Workshop running out of space. Where to next? (S) says next door firm (cloth merchants) is moving out. Why not rent that space?

Edward recognised that the workshop was running out of space. His current capacity was just enough to make a mile of finished cable per day. If he had to make larger quantities of cable, then his current process could be duplicated many times over. The real problem was that there was no space left. Edward decided to discuss the issue with Sybil. To his surprise, she informed him that the cloth merchant next door was on the verge of bankruptcy, in which case Edward could take over the whole premises next door if necessary.

Friday, 25 October 1816
Time to show A & C the new cable production process and the automatic decoding machine.
Reaction was amazement. Both gawped. Both supported the intent to contact Admiralty. Offered partnersip in firm if successful. How and who to contact at Admiralty? Does (S) know? Took the decoder home to show (E) who thought it was magic. Her magic more pleasing.

It was time to let the partners upstairs into his little secret, to wonder at the scope of his idea, and to gawp in amazement at the de-coding machine in operation. For their part, the partners did not let him down: they were suitably amazed and gawped in wonder at the de-coder clicking quietly away, producing a printed message as if by magic. Their reaction was so enthusiastic that they fully endorsed his intention contact the Admiralty, and even offered Edward a partnership in the firm, which left Edward speechless.

That evening he took the de-coder home to show Elsie, who was equally impressed. She couldn't understand how an idea in Edward's head could be made into such a complex piece of machinery. Edward assured her that he personally didn't make the device: he designed and drew the machine on paper and the craftsmen made what he drew. To somebody who was not able to read engineering drawings, the process must have seemed on the verge of magic. According to his cryptic notes, Elsie too had some magic of her own to show him.

Edward freely admits that he had absolutely no idea how to contact the Admiralty, nor indeed who to contact. In this context, his engineering expertise was of no account. The partners upstairs were likewise of no help. In desperation he sought the advice of the oracle of good sense, Sybil.

Monday, 28 October 1816
(S) says be bold. Write to FNL direct. Tell him what you can do for him. Be brief. Don't exaggerate. Offer to demonstrate your claims at our cost. Press benefits hard.

Her advice was to be bold and aim for the top: in other words, write to the First Naval Lord himself. Tell him exactly what you can do for him, in simple, straightforward terms. Make your claims brief and to the point. Offer to demonstrate and prove your claims at his earliest convenience and at your cost. Press home the benefits to him. Only use one side of one page of paper.

Apparently, Edward followed her instructions to the letter and arranged for the letter to be delivered by hand the same day. We do not have a copy of this letter and neither do we have a copy of the reply, but we do know from the notebook that Edward received a reply a week later from the personal aide to the First Naval Lord, Vice-Admiral, Sir Graham Moore. The reply effectively invited Edward to attend an interview with the aide at the Admiralty, where Edward could present his case for further consideration.

Monday 4 November 1816
Aide to FNL replied. Invited for interview. First impressions in business mean a lot. Look sloppy, think sloppy. Must be smart and well prepared. No waffle or piffle. (E)will check I am immaculate.

Rarely in the Project Notebook are there any references to Edward himself, except for one short paragraph where he emphasises his concerns about the impact and importance of first impressions. Edward was neither, a dandy nor a fop, but he did pay great attention his manner of dress and to the detail and quality of cloth and tailoring. It wasn't a matter of vanity, merely an important business precaution. At the time, it was common practice to judge people by first impressions, which persists even to this day. Sloppy in appearance equated with sloppy thinking and sloppy business practice. Edward admits to being very particular about personal hygiene, and dresses in a manner not to be noticed. He preferred being in the background, rather than being the centre of attention. Prior to the arrival of Elsie, he attended to his appearance himself, but since she joined his household it was Elsie who selected his clothes and made sure that his appearance was as immaculate as hers.

Edward favoured a leather external purse, chained to his belt, rather than carrying stuff in his pockets. He preferred long breeches down to his boot tops below the knee. He didn't wear a peri-wig, instead his hair was cut short and dressed with fine perfumed wax. He was clean-shaven (no beard, moustache or sideburns). He always wore clean, white, linen shirts with a plain white neck tie: no frilly or lace cuffs. His only concession to flamboyance was a colourful waistcoat. Normally he wore a formal black jacket with tails at rear. In cold weather, he also wore a topcoat with rabbit fur collar. At first, he often wore a broad brim soft felt hat, but changed this to a short top hat (not a stove pipe). Apart from his fob watch, he wore no other adornments. Essentially, he could easily be missed in a crowd.

Wednesday, 6 November 1816
(E) says I look like Mr Average but smarter. V. cold day. Wore top coat with rabbit collar. Aide very pleasant jovial man, Jerome Ballard. Used first names. Recited my speech, rehearsed yesterday. Stressed good points of optical cables and importance of absolute security. Navy use codebooks, not very secure. Made good impression I think. Demonstrated de-coding machine. Jerry was speechless. Very good impression. Offered 10 mile test demonstration against current Chatham line.

He presented himself at the Admiralty for his appointment with, Lieutenant Jerome Ballard, the aide to the First Naval Lord, Vice-Admiral, Sir Graham Moore. Edward found the young lieutenant most affable and not in the least intimidating. Indeed, he insisted on using first names rather than stuffy titles. Edward had rehearsed what he was going to say in front of Elsie the previous evening.

Edward briefly described what he knew about, and the extent of the French method, and his knowledge of the previous Shutter lines to Chatham, Portsmouth and Plymouth. Edward also emphasised their common weaknesses; the signals were open to the public (and enemies) for all to see, they all depended on the weather and visibility, they were unable to work at night, and they also depended on vigilance with telescopes for long periods.

Immediately, Edward launched into a description of his own system, but this time emphasising how his method overcame every weakness of the previous methods. Moreover, his method would be cheaper to run because there was only half the number of repeater stations.

Firstly, Edward made sure that the young aide recognised the importance of security and the importance of limiting who had access to messages. He also asked if the new telegraph used a signals codebook, and how did the new method send messages in both directions? The young lieutenant was evasive about two-way messages. It was almost as if messages would always be out-bound not in-bound. When Edward pressed for an answer the young man offered the explanation that at a certain point in the day the system worked in reverse, i.e. in-bound messages. This was an inherent weakness, compared to his two-way method. The Home Popham method also worked by assigning numbers to words or phrases, i.e. a code book. It is true that this speeds up the process of sending a message, but the process of encoding a message means hunting through pages and pages of the codebook, even if it is arranged alphabetically.

It was time to present the young man with his impressive de-coding machine, which he produced with a flourish. Edward explained that he had previously prepared a message on paper tape, which he extracted from his pocket, and loaded into the tiny clockwork marvel. He also explained that the original writer of the message would have produced this tape, and that the receiver of the message would have a machine to decode it. Nobody else would have access to the message other than these two people. Edward started his machine while the lieutenant watched in amazement as it chattered quietly and printed out a well-known nursery rhyme.

The young lieutenant was speechless.

To hammer home the point, Edward confirmed that he was willing to demonstrate his method over a ten- mile experiment, at his own expense. He was also willing for the admiralty to use his method as an interim solution while waiting for their signal stations to become operational. He was eager to discuss his proposals with the First Naval Lord himself, to determine where and when the experiment should take place. Edward admits that he was rather proud of the way he had managed the conversation and the interview. At the very least he had sown the seeds of doubt as well as the seeds of salvation. He was confident of a positive reply, but not so confident that it would happen soon. Alacrity and Admiralty rarely occur in the same sentence.

Tuesday, 12 November 1816
It is obvious that the labour content of the filament line: joining, drawing, coating, winding is the same as the 12-filament cable line: shola sticks, cotton tape, bitumen coat, winding. The speed of both is similar, but the filament line uses 12 times more labour. Increasing speed problems are unknown. Duplicate line and share labour across several lines is better.
Labour costs per mile =£10
Materials (glass, cotton, shola, bitumen)=£15
Overheads=£5
Profit=£10
Selling price=£40

Edward privately re-assured himself that his optical cable answered all the weaknesses of any semaphore method, and together with his coding and de-coding machines, his solution was infinitely more secure. He was also satisfied that his current production capacity would be able to meet the demands of his proposed experiment. The notebook records his scribbled calculations of the production cost per mile of his twelve-filament cable, which reveal that the major cost item was not the glass rods, but the labour required to man the production process. A single filament was a paltry sum but all twelve filaments to Portsmouth were more than the annual cost of running the Admiralty semaphore line. The problem lay in the filament making process and not in the cable making process. He couldn't argue with his numbers: the filament process output needed to be doubled at least, with the same labour.

The options were simple; double the speed or duplicate the line. He was reluctant to increase the speed because the current line worked so well. Duplicating the line was a simpler option because it only involved duplicating the glass rod-joining machine. The winding drum part could be easily modified to handle two drums. The original labour cost could also be spread across both production lines.

Cautious Edward had once again solved the problem in his mind. He could now offer a price of 40 pounds per mile or 2880 pounds for the complete cable from London to Portsmouth (72 miles). His main advantage was that his running costs would be less than half the running costs of the Admiralty line. Edward also roughly estimated the cost of erecting posts for the cable, with a ten-man team laying two miles per day, as 10 pounds per day including posts and wire. These costs did not include renting space for his seven repeater stations. His opinion was that the Admiralty should provide the space or pay the rents.

It seems that Edward was blessed with foresight, because surprisingly, within a couple of days a letter was delivered to him personally, advising him that the Semaphore committee at the Admiralty required his presence, accompanied by his equipment, to discuss telegraphic communications. Edward promptly wrote a note to Jerry Ballard confirming his acceptance.

THE ADMIRALTY

On the morning of the big day, Edward arrived at work earlier than usual and packed a leather satchel with a coder and de-coder and a short length of cable with brass couplings at each end. He contemplated taking an Argand lamp with him, but decided against it, because he assumed that the Navy must have such lamps of their own.

Wednesday, 20 November 1816
Meeting with FNL plus five admirals (semaphore committee).
Jerry pre-warned me not to disagree with FNL.
Interim telegraph service*
Explained cyphers – importance of security*
10 mile test cable (Chatham line)*
Running cost of cable – half semaphore cost.
Saving £2000 over 2 years. Could fund Portsmouth line?
Navy Intelligence
V. Impressive demonstration. *
Cable can do code books*
Comments – new semaphore no better than unreliable shutter line?
Chatham demonstration accepted*

FNL v interested in cypher machines.
Firm now under Naval Secrets – also self as Lietenant.
All devices top secret. Rank and record of officer killed in
Dardanelles Action. Not suitable for active service. Am I at
risk? My ideas too valuable and dangerous. Part time advisor to
FNL assigned to Communication branch, Naval Intelligence.
Must wear uniform at meetings. Dumbfounded! Discuss with
(S) and (E).

Edward's notebook does not give us a full account of the meeting; instead there are a series of headings with asterisks or question marks that presumably indicate whether he thought he had made his point or whether he had not done so. His notebook does tell us that prior to the meeting, the aide, Lieutenant Ballard, pre-warned Edward not to disagree with the First Naval Lord, who apparently could not abide dissent. In addition to the First Naval Lord, there were five other admirals or vice-admirals as well as the aide, who took minutes of the meeting. We do not have copies of these minutes, so I have assumed that what transpired is roughly as follows:

As chairman, the First Naval Lord, introduced himself and the other committee members to Edward. He then announced his understanding of the previous meeting between Edward and his aide, and asked Edward to confirm that this was a fair account. He went on to detail which parts were of interest to the committee; namely an interim telegraph service, while their own semaphore stations became operational, and Edward's

96

views on secret cyphers and whether his equipment could accommodate the existing Navy code books.

Edward responded by thanking the First Naval Lord and the committee for allowing him the opportunity to present his case for their consideration. It is likely that Edward praised or congratulated them for recognising the weaknesses of all semaphore methods, and for recognising that his method solved all these problems. It is also more than likely that Edward made them aware that neither he nor his company were wealthy enough to fund a cable from London to Portsmouth from their own pockets, but they were prepared to lay a ten-mile test cable between two stations on the current line to Chatham. He would have pointed out that the running costs of his method would be half the cost of the new semaphore line resulting in a saving of over three thousand pounds over two years. This sum itself would be enough to fund the laying of the Portsmouth cable.

He would have laid the foundation arguments for the success of the Navy being dependent on the quality and quantity of its intelligence. Intelligence: meaning information about and the intentions of its enemies. If the Admiralty didn't already have a department that was tasked with managing intelligence, then it needed to think seriously about doing so. He probably endorsed this idea with a subtle suggestion that the gentlemen present had already perceived this reality and that such a department had probably been in operation for some time, otherwise why would they be concerned with replacing the old shutter line to Portsmouth? A high speed signalling method that delivered intelligence from ships at sea obviously did not yet exist, but as soon as the ship docked, is was of the utmost importance to deliver whatever intelligence it possessed to the Admiralty as quickly and secretly as possible, so that the gentlemen charged with giving the orders, could transmit those orders back the ships as quickly as possible, into the hands of brave captains to enact.

There is no doubt that Edward would have confirmed that his cable method was infinitely more secure than any semaphore method, and that his cable could handle any coding method including the existing codebook. There was every likelihood that Edward would have hammered home the advantages of his coding and de-coding machines, followed by an impressive demonstration. I would guess that this probably involved teaching the young aide how to send a simple message while Edward pretended to be a receiver.

Using a code book would not be a problem for Edward's machines, because code books convert letters, words or phrases into numbers. Edward's machines could switch between alphabetical letters or numbers with ease. The principal weakness of the code book method is that if the enemy obtains a copy of the code book, for example; the enemy could capture a ship to obtain the code book, then this renders the code open to the enemy. His own method used many different codes which could be changed daily. The header line on a message indicated which code was to be used to decode that message. He considered this to be a far more flexible and secure method.

Whatever the form of the demonstration, it must have impressed the committee, because they accepted his offer of a demonstration between two stations on the Chatham line, where both methods could be compared side by side. They also accepted that the test could be funded from what remained in the semaphore account, and they still had the option whether to complete the semaphore line or not. Some were clearly opposed to completing the line because it would be no better than the former unreliable 'shutter line'.

In the case of the cypher machines, the First Naval Lord expressed a profound interest, whereas the others considered these machines to be part and parcel of Edward's telegraph, and didn't look beyond at the wider implications of mechanised coding. Obviously, the First Naval Lord did appreciate the wider implications and insisted that Edward should stay behind after the meeting closed.

His Lordship was surprisingly frank with Edward when they were alone, which took Edward off-guard. It appears that his Lordship praised Edward for not attempting to Patent his devices. As of this moment, they were henceforth under the umbrella of Admiralty secrets.

Although the crown, the navy and the military had been engaged in espionage for centuries, dating back to Elizabeth I in the 16th century, the modern age of government secrecy didn't begin until a century later when the wide-ranging Official Secrets Act of 1911 became law.

In Edward's time, the Law relating to Admiralty secrets required that a potential offender had to be a legitimate navy contractor or a serving member of the Navy. To avoid any confusion about his status, his Lordship informed Edward that his firm would be classified as a civilian contractor and he would hold the rank of Lieutenant in His Majesty's Navy. In effect, Edward would be under oath, legally and professionally, not to divulge the nature of his work to anyone. Edward was on the point of objecting because his brother had been killed in action while serving for the navy, but he remembered the aide's warning, so he kept silent. His Lordship stressed that his rank was purely a technical arrangement and that he would not be called for active duty: he was far too valuable to be exposed to the risk of capture by our enemies.

It was clear that his Lordship was acutely aware of the nature of Naval Intelligence and the need for utmost secrecy, because he informed Edward that he would be assuming the Service Record and rank of a recent casualty of the Dardanelles Operation. His Service Record would be marked 'not suitable for further active duty – now assigned to Communications branch of Naval Intelligence'. Edward had suddenly acquired two identities: a Navy lieutenant and a civilian instrument engineer. For obvious reasons the notebook does not reveal the name of his Navy persona, nor the ship that he served on. Past newspapers revealed that the Navy suffered 29 deaths and 138 injured. The Dardanelles Operation was described as ill-fated and inadequate.

His Lordship went on to explain his reasoning, that Edward's ideas and his machines could or would revolutionise the use and complexity of cyphers. The Navy could not afford for Edward to work for any other nation: his knowledge was far too dangerous to fall into the hands of potential enemies. The Navy had to have Edward on their side in whatever capacity, provided he didn't share his knowledge with anyone else. He would of course be paid for his services, which in turn allowed the Navy to forcibly restrict his activities elsewhere. His Lordship told Edward that he would draw up a legal contract, which he expected Edward to sign, because he was both sensible and intelligent.

At that time, the organisation and administration of Naval Intelligence was the responsibility of the First Naval Lord. In the first instance, it was his intention to establish a restructured office of Naval Intelligence, which would have two branches; the first was signals and communications, and the second was the compilation and distribution of intelligence. Edward would be assigned to the communications branch. To ensure Edward's anonymity, his Lordship expected Edward to use his new identity and to dress appropriately: at the Admiralty nobody stands out more than people in civilian attire.

Ostensibly he would continue with his present occupation, under his own name, and would assist the Admiralty on a part-time basis. His immediate task would be to review all Navy communications with a view to improving their security and reliability, working directly for the First Naval Lord.

Edward remarks in the notebook that he was dumbfounded by his Lordship's observations. He has secured a probable long-lasting contract for his firm and now had a second paid job with the Admiralty. It was ironic that his brother, Thomas, had worked hard for many years to achieve the rank of able seaman, and yet Edward had exceeded that rank in an afternoon. He was not entirely happy that the Navy could forcibly restrict his activities, but he would need to see the contract before raising any objections.

Back at his office Edward called a meeting with Sybil and the partners upstairs to inform them of what had transpired at the Admiralty. He had secured a ten-mile test of the cable and a probable long-term contract for the coding and de-coding machines. The Admiralty had also declared that these machines were 'secret', so all relevant drawings must now be locked away. At the same time Edward had been classified as a lieutenant, which meant that the firm now had a permanent man on the inside at the Admiralty. In a stoke, Edward had secured the future prosperity of the firm, at least for the time being.

Edward couldn't get home quickly enough to share his good news with Elsie. He insisted that she should accompany him to Firmins in the Strand where he would be outfitted with a naval lieutenant's uniform, complete with cocked hat. On the journey back home, it seems that Elsie was tearful because she was afraid that Edward looked so dashing and handsome that someone else might steal his affections. He assured her that this would not happen, but Elsie was not easily persuaded until much later that night.

The notebook doesn't say so, but I would guess that Elsie was more than a little perturbed by the ominous, veiled threat delivered by the First Naval Lord. Obviously, his Lordship chose his words diplomatically, but essentially what he was saying to Edward was that Edward's ideas and inventions were potentially so dangerous that Great Britain could not afford for him to work for any other nation. The inference here is that, if he was not prepared to work for the nation, then he would be prevented from working for anybody else. In technical terms, Edward was brilliant, but politically he was naïve. The problem for Edward was that he could not undo his imagination or ignore his genius. The problem for his Lordship was that he couldn't undo his imagination either. In the circumstances his Lordship had made the only decision open to him: to employ Edward's genius for the benefit of the nation, and to keep him well hidden and well protected against other nations. At least this solution had a good chance of working bearing in mind the secretive nature of Edward's work.

Probably, Edward was completely unaware of the direction that the First Naval Lord's mind was working. After all, Edward's forte was reality and practicality: supposition and speculation were not included in his repertoire.

Optics Notebook
Edward B. Raine
General Manager
Thursday, 21 November 1816
Promooted to full partner with office upstairs. Signboard repainted. Chief designer and General Manager. Same as usual.

The most visible outcome of Edward's meeting with the Admiralty was that he was promoted to a full partner in the business, with his name added to the signboard above the entrance to the premises. He was also assigned an office upstairs. He also changed the name of his 'Workshop Notebook' to 'Optics Notebook' In all other respects, the firm carried on as usual.

THE CHATHAM TEST

Monday, 25 November 1816
Letters arrived from Admiralty to confirm Chatham test.
Personal letter reference my officer's commision and letter of
Authority and access to all parts of navy.
(S) advises sending contracts to our lawyers.

True to his word, Sir Graham Moore arranged for the Admiralty Civilian Contracts branch to send Edward two contracts. The first was addressed to Ayres and Compton and referred to the ten-mile demonstration cable. The second was a personal commission addressed to Lieutenant Edward Raine, which detailed his duties and remuneration. Attached to his commission was a handwritten authorisation bearing the First Naval Lord's signature and his seal. The authorisation named Edward as Naval Intelligence (Communications Branch) Chief Investigator reporting directly to the First Naval Lord. In effect this allowed him access to any part of the British Navy.

Nowadays, Edward routinely consulted Sybil whenever contracts of any sort were involved. Invariably she suggested that the firm should use their normal lawyers to peruse the documents to ensure that the firm were not committing themselves to undue risks. She also suggested that Edward should do the same with his commission. Sybil even suggested that she could take the short walk to Lincolns Inn to deliver the documents.

Wednesday, 27 November 1816
Letters by hand – replies to Admiralty contracts.
Not specific enough about passing Chatham test.
My commission not clear enough. Time spent. No exclusion from active duty. Where do I work? No duration or limits.
Consulted (S). Composed letters to FNL making detailed points about Chatham test (Kennington to Shooters hill). Composition of test messages. Day and night. Need adjudicator. Date set for 30 days time (after Christmas).
Personal commission revisions. Number of days/ month. Suggested 2. Duration, suggested retirement/ 65 age. Workplace – Admiralty. Active duty excluded, brother killed in action 1794 (HMS Alexander).

The lawyers responded with unusual haste, recommending that a date should be agreed with the Admiralty and added to the cable contract. They also suggested that the terms of the test needed to be much more explicit, so that both sides will be able to recognise when the test has been passed or has failed.

Edward's commission attracted a good deal more comment from the lawyers. The notebook only has brief references to their objections; the number of hours or days per month was not specified, there was no mention of exclusion from active duty, there was no mention of where Edward was expected to work, and there was no mention of the duration of his commission.

Once more Edward was obliged to consult Sybil, who spent some hours composing a conciliatory reply; not too apologetic and not too demanding. She also suggested a date for the cable test 30 days hence, and the locations as the Kennington station (relatively close to Norwood) and the nearest semaphore station ten miles towards Chatham at Shooters Hill. The test itself could consist of 100 words, with each word composed of five random letters and/or numbers. The test would be in two parts; sending messages from Kennington to the remote station, and then sending messages from the remote station to Kennington. One test would be conducted in daylight, and a second test at midnight. Lieutenant Raine would personally train two teams of Navy officers to use the coding and de-coding machines. The navy would supply a third officer at each location as the adjudicator. Each adjudicator must be in possession of a copy of the original messages so that they can verify the accuracy of the telegraph test. Alternatively, the same message can be re-sent back to Kennington, in which case only one adjudicator would be required.

In the case of Edward's commission, she suggested a maximum of two days per week or the equivalent, e.g. eight days per month with a termination date when Edward reached 65 years of age or death, whichever occurred first. The remuneration should be reviewed annually. Sybil also felt that Edward should mention his reluctance to engage in 'active' service, because his brother had been killed in November 1794 in a battle with the French, off the coast of France, while serving aboard HMS Alexander under Rear Admiral Richard Bligh. Sybil was confident that Edward was at no risk of being called to active service, but she felt it was a sensible legal precaution to establish this fact at the outset.

Wednesday 4 December 1816
Contract letters sent last week. Suggestions agreed and confirmed today by Admiralty. Now that I am in the Navy the workmen jest by saying Aye, Aye Sir. Is a joke now, but I hope it wears off soon..

The notebook records that these letters were sent, and that a week later the Admiralty confirmed the suggestions relating to the ten-mile test and those concerning his commission. The notebook also mentions that, in jest, the workshop saluted Edward and addressed him as captain, and often used the expression 'aye, aye Sir'.

Tuesday, 10 December 1816
Wrote to Jerry Ballard to confirm cable was ready for test. Cable will be supported on temporary post along Rocheter turnpike. I will connect coding and de-coding machines on day before. 2 days before (S) and self will train users at Admiralty. I will attend at Kennington and (S) will attend at Shooters Hill

– staying at The Bull. Admiralty agreed to send back message from Shooters Hill to Kennington, so only one adjudicator needed.

Two weeks later, Edward wrote to Lieutenant Ballard to inform him that the cable had been manufactured and his workmen were ready to lay the test cable. For the most part, the cable would be supported on temporary posts alongside the Rochester turnpike. On the day before the test, Edward would personally connect the two coding and de-coding machines at each end of the cable. Two days before the test, Edward and his assistant would present themselves at the Admiralty to train the officers who would operate the machines. On the day of the test, Edward, would be present at the Kennington station, while his assistant, Mrs Sybil Thorton, would be present at Shooters Hill. He added that Mrs Thorton would have a room at the Bull Tavern close to the semaphore station. The notebook also records that it took the gang of four workmen two days to lay the cable, working from both ends at the same time. The glass-blowers acted as supervisors and later, stayed overnight at the Bull. There is no mention of any problems with laying the cable.

Prior to the test, Edward and a very nervous Sybil made their way to the Admiralty. Despite her initial nervousness, Sybil excelled during the training session. Edward comments that Sybil quickly adopted her 'teacher mode' and strangely the young officers assumed the role of eager students. Women were obviously not frequent visitors to this very male oriented establishment, but the Navy took it all in their stride. For her part, Sybil drilled the officers so well that they could virtually recite their instructions by heart. Sybil was quick to commend them all for being such good learners, and so proficient with the machines. Edward was most impressed with her performance and noted that she had a natural gift.

Thursday, 2 January 1817
Chatham test today.
Met adjudicator (retired Capt.)
(S) travelled alone to Shooters Hill.
Hand printed message sheet 100 words, 5 letters per word in 4 columns. Sent in 25 mins. (semaphore took 75 minutes).
Sent ready signal and Shooters Hill returned the same message. Paper tape inserted in decoder. Adjudicator says Perfect. Sent message to (S). Congratulations.
Very good dinner (with much ale) then waited for midnight.
Repeated previous test with new message. 25 mins and 10 seconds. No semaphore working. Message sent back from Shooters Hill and decoded in 16 minutes. Took adjudicator 60 minutes to check. Perfect again. Sent (S) messsage Perfect again meet you tomorrow.

On the day of the test, it was Edward's turn to be nervous, whereas Sybil seemed completely composed, at least outwardly. On the coach ride to Kennington Edward enquired if Sybil required him to travel with her to the Bull tavern, but she replied that she was more

111

than capable of managing on her own. The adjudicator (a retired captain) handed the young officer a beautifully printed sheet of four columns of 'words'. Edward stood behind the young man as he started to send the test messages, with one hand on the young man's shoulder. As the officer completed each set of twenty-five words, Edward tapped his hand and muttered words of encouragement. In less than 25 minutes the young man had sent all 100 'words'. At the time, Edward was not aware that the semaphore station was also sending the same message. Later he learnt that it took more than three times longer to send the same message by semaphore.

The Admiralty had accepted Edward's suggestion to re-send the same message back to Kennington. The young officer at the machine signalled 'ready' and the sender at Shooters Hill began the return message. A few seconds under 25 minutes the message ended, so Edward extracted the paper tape, wound up the clockwork engine and put it into the de-coder. In just over sixteen minutes, the decoder stopped chattering. Edward extracted the tape and presented it to the adjudicator to verify, which took an hour. With a smile, the adjudicator announced that the paper tape agreed perfectly with the original message. Previously, Edward and Sybil had agreed to send her a message announcing the outcome of the test, so Edward instructed the officer to send 'Congratulations perfect'.

Edward entertained the young officer and the adjudicator to a hearty dinner at a nearby tavern until shortly before midnight. Sybil had been instructed to do the same. At the stroke of midnight, the machine at Kennington received the 'ready' signal, so another test was conducted with a different set of test words. This time the semaphore arms remained silent. The transmission took ten seconds longer than the morning test, and similarly the return message took slightly longer. The de-coder machine chattered away for sixteen minutes and then fell silent. The adjudicator took well over an hour (probably the effects of alcohol) to confirm that the return message matched the original perfectly. Once again Edward sent a message to Sybil 'Perfect again meet you tomorrow'. She would sleep easy that night.

Friday, 3 January 1817
Wrote to Jerry to thank him for his help and guidance.
Celebrated successful test in workshop. Thanked everybody.
(E) very excited., full of praise.

Back at work the following day, Edward wrote to Lieutenant Ballard, thanking him for all his help and assistance, and then joined the rest of the workshop celebrating the success of the tests the previous day. It seems that Sybil had arranged extra rations and ale. The result of their efforts was that the firm now had two new products with no immediate competition. Prosperity was on the horizon and beckoning.

THE ROYAL NAVY

Later, on the Monday, a letter arrived from Jerome Ballard informing Edward that the First Naval Lord had requested his presence at a meeting the following day.

We can only imagine the reception that Edward received from Elsie that night. She had not seen Edward for two days and was probably eager to find out what had happened during the important tests. No doubt Edward re-assured her about the tests and about how much he missed her. The notebook makes no reference to these matters, except that he felt exceedingly cheerful the following day.

Monday 6 January 1817
Meeting at the Admiralty to review tests.
Checked uniform and cocked hat with Jerry.
FNL says tests were flawless.
3 immediate tasks:
Check all communication procedures at all ports. And possible cable connections to all (3 months – needs visits)
Report all possible methods of ship-ship and ship-shore signals. Cables not the answer. Flags and pennants in the meantime. (2 months interim)
Report unbreakable cod methods. (1 month)
Afternoon back at work – pretended I was Captain at the helm – look lively lads. At home (E) says I know more about codes than books do. Are unbreakable codes possible? Perhaps very

complex codes are sufficient. Takes too long to break. Caution – using broken code intelligence is dangerous..

I think we can safely assume that Elsie fussed over Edward on the morning of his meeting with the First Naval Lord. I think we can also assume that Edward consulted Lieutenant Ballard about his uniform, how to wear his cocked hat and his overall appearance before the meeting.

His Lordship began by congratulating Edward on the flawless tests the previous day, and then proceeded to outline three important tasks that he had in mind for Edward: to report on all communications activities at all Navy ports throughout the kingdom, and to draw up a scheme to connect them all to the Admiralty by his cable. He was also charged with reporting on various possible methods of ship-to-shore and ship-to-ship communications. His Lordship also wanted Edward's views on the most secure way of communicating with unbreakable codes.

Edward commented that it would probably take about three months to complete the first task because he would need to visit all the current establishments. The last task would take about a month to complete, whereas the second task was so speculative that he couldn't put an estimate on when he could expect to complete it, although he could certainly produce an interim report in two months. His Lordship reminded

Edward that he had his personal authority to carry out these investigations, and that he would be fully reimbursed for any expenses incurred by way of travel, lodging and victuals. The meeting was short and to the point. Clearly his Lordship had no time for pleasantries or idle chatter. Within the hour Edward was on his way to the workshop in Leadenhall Street, still dressed in his full Navy regalia.

When he arrived, Sybil was full of praise, but the workmen made endless humorous comments, but they were harmless rather than derisive. He even stood before the wooden winding drum, as if it was the helm, and shouted to the workmen to 'look lively, lads'.

Back at home, Edward tried to explain to Elsie that he was completely in the dark about what the Admiralty did or didn't know about secret codes. Secret codes are secret. Nobody talks about such things. The stuff of his imagination didn't come from reading books: he was not even aware that any books had ever been written about secret codes. For all he knew he was breaking new ground. Elsie didn't need to be told: she knew that her Edward was a genius. If books were ever written about the subject, it would her Edward that would write them.

What nagged at Edward's brain was the thought that, so far, he had only considered different methods of creating codes, but he was also aware of their weaknesses. He had not yet thought of an unbreakable code. It was true that a combination of his ideas could produce excessively difficult codes, but could they be classified as unbreakable? His brain immediately took up another thread: perhaps an unbreakable code was impossible. Surely, given infinite time and resources, good luck and good guesswork, then any code could be broken. It was certainly a possibility that exceptionally complex codes were, 'for all practical purposes', unbreakable. Essentially, if it took so long to attempt to break a code then it might be too late to take any appropriate action. Perhaps this would be the most practical basis for the analysis for his Lordship. He needed to commit his thoughts to paper and to reason the logic more analytically, because he felt that somewhere amongst these ramblings were profoundly important principles.

Code books, by their very nature, were extremely difficult to break. Even if the words and phrases in the code book are arranged in alphabetical order, the code numbers associated with the text could be quite random and arbitrary. Breaking such code books verges on the impossible. However, code books are the most vulnerable to theft or copying. Once a code book gets into the hands of a potential enemy, then all the existing books must be destroyed and a whole new set had to be printed and distributed. In this context, Edward's advice to the Navy would be to routinely attempt to steal or copy the code books used by other nations, while at the same time, keeping their own code books under lock and key.

These thoughts prompted Edward to ask the rhetorical question, 'if we were able to intercept enemy messages, what would we do with the information?'. Clearly if we react to all the intercepted messages, then our enemies will become suspicious. One or two defeats here and there can be put down to bad luck, but a whole succession would smell 'fishy'. Again, Edward's advice to the Navy would be to exercise restraint and caution about using broken codes too often. In this context, he also recommended that our own Navy should routinely send false messages to check whether their own codes had been breached.

The Optics notebook is far less explicit about these thoughts. It was Edward's custom to make lists of headings to remind himself of his train of thought, rather than write out the fine detail.

Whilst Edward was prepared to acknowledge that code books were effectively unbreakable, he was most concerned about their vulnerability. At the same time, he also recognized that his own 'needle' discs were no more than simple substitution codes, which he already knew were prone to 'letter frequency' analysis. However, a simple ratchet mechanism on the disc could easily change the current substitution codes with each successive letter. If the ratchet allowed the steel disc to move one position relative to the brass disc, then 31 letters later, the code would start to repeat itself. In practice the ratchet converted one disc into 31 discs, which Edward felt ought to be enough to defeat any attempt at letter frequency analysis. Who would have thought that a simple ratchet would make such a difference to the complexity of a code? If the sending and receiving stations had a library of a dozen or so different discs, then this would further increase the number of different code combinations.

He also knew that his 'scrambling' idea would be difficult to convert to a simple mechanical device and could only be done by the sender or the recipient. The intermediate repeater stations would not be involved. He decided to keep this device in reserve in case he was requested to improve his current process towards being 'unbreakable' for all practical purposes. The current process was secure, simple and elegant, and he didn't want to add any other cumbersome pieces of equipment.

THE GRAND TOUR

Monday, 20 January 1917
Began tour of Navy docks. Surprised at 500 tom Myrmidon, 20 gun sloop. Expected small cutter. Jerry has been told to take care of me. Overdone. Good company, but do I need a bodyguard? No seasickness. Nosey Capt. Henry Leeke. Asked what I did. Missed Sheerness (boatyard only). Docked at Chatham. Met commanding officer, Sir Charles Rowley. Semaphore officer who complained that semaphore too often held up by poor visibility. Code book symbols very time consuming. Code book not locked away.

Edward began his tour of the principal Navy establishments at Greenwich in the pleasant, jovial company of Jerry Ballard. Edward was convinced that his companion had been dispatched to keep an eye on the inexperienced Edward to make sure that he did nothing foolish. It was like having a personal bodyguard. Edward expected to sail in something small, like a cutter, so he was very surprised to board the Myrmidon, a 500 ton, 120-foot, 20-gun sloop, with 18 carronades and a crew of 135, under the command of Captain Henry Leeke. Jerry joked that the First Naval Lord had issued instructions to take very good care of the young Lieutenant. Edward's comment was that the Navy had over-done this instruction.

The Captain's instructions were to ferry the two Lieutenants to each of the Navy establishments between Chatham and Falmouth, and then to proceed to the Africa station. It seems that the ship was only five years old, and the Commander gave them a brief history of the ship's activities since its launch. The Captain then gently enquired what the purpose was for their visits. Jerry replied that he was the aide to the First Naval Lord and was carrying confidential messages to the officers in command at each establishment.

The Commander nodded sagely, and then asked Edward, "So what do you do?" Edward could have lied and used the same excuse as Jerry, but he decided that a limited version of the truth would be easier to defend, "I work directly for the First Naval Lord in the communications branch of Naval Intelligence," admitted Edward putting a finger to his lips to indicate that this was confidential information. The Captain whispered back, "Yes, but what do you actually do?" Edward very calmly replied, "I make sure that messages to and from the Admiralty, start off as secrets and remain that way until they reach their destination. You could say that it is my job to make sure that our enemies and their spies do not find out what we are up to". The Captain's response was, "Oh, very secret then!" Jerry smiled faintly and nodded. The Captain showed them to their cabins, and prudently invited them to dine with him and his officers in his cabin. Obviously these two very young, 'green' officers had the ear of the highest of the high, and for the sake of his own reputation he should treat them graciously.

They made good time to the Thames estuary where the sea was choppy. Despite the conditions Edward was not embarrassed with sea-sickness as they turned south towards Sheerness at the mouth of the Medway. According to Jerry's itinerary, they were not scheduled to stop there because it was basically a ship building base, which was so close to Chatham that they would use the Chatham semaphore if they ever needed to send urgent messages.

When they disembarked at Chatham, they were met by a young lieutenant who escorted them to be introduced to the Commanding Officer, Admiral Sir Charles Rowley, where Edward produced his letter of authority from his Lordship, the First Naval Lord. The elderly but very affable, Sir Charles, enquired about the purpose of their visit, and Edward replied that he wanted to interview the officers in charge of dispatches and the semaphore line to review and seek their opinions on how they made decisions and did their jobs. The Admiral spoke to the young lieutenant, who escorted them to the office of dispatches and later to the semaphore tower. Edward discovered that the two officers in charge worked well together to sort out those messages that could be sent by semaphore and those that had to be delivered by riders (such as sealed messages). The semaphore officer commented that the mechanism was simple and worked well, but poor visibility kept the tower idle too often. He also commented that converting messages to code book symbols was very time consuming. In answer to Edward's query, the officer told him that the code book was kept in a cupboard in the tower. Edward concluded his business and then the lieutenant escorted them back to the Admiral to bid him farewell, before returning to the ship, where they spent the night until the wind changed.

Edward slept well but was awakened by people shouting. On reflection, people were always shouting, morning, noon and night. He asked Jerry if it was always like this onboard ship, and Jerry confirmed that it was so. He also asked Jerry if it was possible to get some water to shave, and Jerry told him that the bosun was the right man to ask. Within minutes a pitcher of steaming water arrived in his cabin. He felt much better and ate a hearty breakfast. He commented to Jerry that the Navy feeds its men well. Jerry smiled and replied, "At least the officers are well fed".

Wednesday, 22 January 1817
Spent the night aboard waiting for good wind. Started at dawn. B/fast good. Jerry says officers are well fed. Arrived Portsmouth late afternoon dusk. Spent eveinng in Portsea mostly taverns. Very jolly. Night onboard. Much shouting. Met Commanding Officer, Sir Edward Thornborough in morning. Jerry not feeling well. Interviewed semaphore officer, disgruntled. Disliked shutter method. Not keen on new method.

Too unreliable (visibilty). Code book tedious. Codebook in unlocked cupboard. Often use riders or ships for urgent messages. Afternoon left for Devnport.

They arrived at Portsmouth in the late afternoon (dusk), and as before, they were escorted and presented to Admiral Sir Edward Thornborough, the commanding officer. After explaining the purpose of their visit, Jerry suggested that they should postpone their interviews until the morning. At the invitation of the very elderly Admiral, they dined with him that evening, and later at Jerry's invitation the two crossed to Portsea to sample several taverns and many jugs of ale.

Despite a disturbed night onboard the ship, Edward awoke refreshed. Jerry was not so fortunate and complained of a headache. Regardless, they began their interviews. Unlike Chatham, dispatches and semaphore messages were under a single, disgruntled officer, who complained that his post was locally considered as a punishment for wayward officers. However, he did have experience of the old 'shutter' telegraph, of which he was highly critical. He was not looking forwards to operating the new Home-Popham system either, simply because it was so dependant on visibility, even if the new system had superior mechanisms. The problem was not the mechanism, it was the weather. He also mentioned that using the code book had been exceedingly tedious. Edward noted that the old 'shutter' code book was kept in an unlocked cupboard. A new code book had not yet been issued. Unlike Chatham, this officer didn't have to make decisions about how to send messages to the Admiralty; everything urgent was sent by riders and everything else went by ships sailing to London. By the early afternoon, they had thanked the Admiral and were back onboard heading for Devonport (Plymouth).

Thursday, 23 January 1817
Much shouting again. Is it always so noisy onboard? Sea rough today. No seasickness. Met Sir Edward Pellew, CO at Devonport. Dined at Admiralty House on the Mount. Very entertaining with stories of sea battles. Unstoppable. Seems Falmouth is often first port of call for ships after long voyages. Mentioned HMS Pickle and dispaches about death of Nelson. Officer in charge of dispatches says nothing is urgent. Ships or riders take 3 days. No previous experience with shutter telegraph but has poor reputation. Codebook on the table. Kept in unlocked cupboard (old shutter code book). Who is responsible for dispatches at Falmouth?
HMS myrmidon has sailed to Africa. Wind from the east so Jerry and self will take the mail coach. V. slow but good chance to see old shutter line. Jerry jested that we challenge the 37 hours by the officer from HMS Pickle. I declined. Good to see (E) again. Exhausted. Fell asleep in her arms. Slept well. Work as usual.

Meanwhile the sea had turned rougher, but still Edward felt no sea-sickness, probably because he was so immersed in writing his reports in between incessant shouting from the crew.

At Devonport, the same welcome procedure was followed, just like Chatham and Portsmouth. Eventually they were introduced to Admiral Sir Edward Pellew, the Commanding Officer. Once again, they dined with the Admiral, at his invitation, at Admiralty House on Mount Wise. Jerry engaged the Admiral about his famous Sack of Algiers, although he later regretted opening the conversation, because once the Admiral got started on his illustrious career, there was no stopping him. One point in the conversation did ring alarm bells for Edward. The admiral mentioned that Falmouth was the first port of call for many Navy ships returning to England. Indeed, it was where HMS Pickle had come ashore with dispatches announcing the death of Lord Nelson at Trafalgar.

Like Portsmouth, there was only one officer in charge of dispatches. However, in his case, there was no such thing as urgent: all messages would take several days by mail coach overland or by ship. What mattered was which direction the wind was blowing. A fast ship and a favourable wind could be faster than the mail coach. This officer had no experience of the previous shutter line, but he recalled that it had a very poor reputation due to the variable weather and was only ever operational one or two days a week. Edward noted that the old 'shutter' code book was on the table. It appears the code book was normally kept in an unlocked cupboard in the office. The officer also made no mention of dispatches that landed at Falmouth. Who was responsible for those?

By the time they had finished interviewing the officer, their ship, the Myrmidon had already sailed for the Africa station. They already knew that the return trip to London was going to be slow. They had two choices, a ship or the mail chaise. Jerry checked the wind direction (from the east) which decided for them. The return would have to be a grueling 200 miles or more on the turnpike. Jerry even jested that they could attempt to break the record set by Lieutenant John Richards Lapenotière in November 1805, who dashed to London, with dispatches announcing the death of Lord Nelson, in 37 hours and 21 stops to change horses, at a cost of 47 pounds. Edward declined the race, even though he was missing the company of Elsie. Much of the coach route would follow the route of the previous 'shutter' telegraph line, which Edward wanted to see anyway, because it would give him some idea of what obstacles his cable would have to contend with. Four and a half days later Edward arrived back home exhausted, and fell asleep, still in his uniform, in the arms of Elsie. The following day he returned to Leadenhall Street, still exhausted, but much happier as he slipped into comfortable, familiar routines.

THE REPORTS

Tuesday, 28 January 1817
Bitterly cold. Need (S) to help with reports. Unfair to involve her or (E). Supposed to be secret work. Remind them of secret work. Thought about ship-shore signals. Don't know of any solution. Certainly not cables. Optical cable has 10 mile limit. Cannot cross oceans. Much brighter light source perhaps 100 miles would be great help. Could cover nation and Ireland and Belgium ports. Still not global. No indication that science has the answer. In the meantime it is flags or nothing. Most likely electric cables will win over optics because relays can boost signals with no human intervention. Sent reports to FNL by hand immediately. None of it good news but all true and fair.

Normally before committing anything to paper, Edward was in the habit of consulting Sybil for advice, but in this case, he remembered that he was now working in the realm of Admiralty secrets. He didn't feel at all comfortable about involving Sybil, nor Elsie for that matter. They were innocents and must remain so. The subject matter of the first two of his three reports he had to write, were very clearly secret. He had no qualms about discussing isolated fragments about his machine designs, to clarify his own thoughts, but anything directly related to Admiralty matters would have to remain off-limits. His notebook mentions that he must remember to speak to Elsie and Sybil about this restriction.

While Edward was in the mood, he put his mind to the final speculative report concerning ship-to-shore and ship-to-ship communications. His first observation was that the Royal Navy, like the British Empire encompassed the whole globe. Even a shore-shore cable that stretched around the world, would still have to cross the Atlantic and the Pacific oceans. Currently his cable required repeater stations at 10-mile intervals, which ruled out using his cable across the oceans. This limitation was imposed by the feeble source of initial illumination. What Edward needed was a much brighter source, more like sunlight, although as a temporary measure he would accept any bright source that could travel 100 miles.

If that was possible, then the whole nation, including Ireland, could be connected by optical cable with a handful of repeater stations. Indeed, the Belgian port of Oostende would also be within reach, and from there the cable could extend to the Mediterranean and onwards to India and Africa, and perhaps Australia too. To encourage scientific research into bright light sources, perhaps the Admiralty might be persuaded to offer a prize, just as they did with the nautical chronometer, (such a prize would soon have been won, with limelight, by Goldsworthy Gurney in 1825 or Thomas Drummond 1826). Such a cable running through Russia could connect to America across the narrow (51 miles) Bearing Straits. Once in America, the cable could run all the way to the southern tip of Chile, and at some point, branch eastwards to the Caribbean. Just a nominal improvement to 100-mile repeater intervals would make all this possible.

As far as he was aware, there were no known scientific methods of transmitting signals across vast distances. The closest he knew about was sunlight (the heliograph was not invented until much later in the century). Atmospheric conditions on Earth would probably limit even sunlight to perhaps 100 miles, provided the transmitting point was at least 6725 feet above sea level, to overcome the curvature of the Earth. At least his cable was immune from the elements. Even if mountains of that height could be found close to shore, he still had no idea how to convert a single point of light to send messages (Morse code had not been invented at that time).

Edward knew of nothing on the scientific horizon that remotely resembled unlimited global transmission, (he would have to wait until the end of the century before Guglielmo Marconi managed to transmit radio waves across the Atlantic). Until such a discovery was invented, the problems of ship-to-ship and ship-to-shore would remain in the hands of flags or pennants over very short distances. In his opinion, optical cables, or any other types of cable, were not the right solution.

To his credit Edward was scrupulously fair in his analysis and admitted that electrical cables had a significant advantage over optical cables in that electrical repeater stations to boost the signal strength did not need human intervention like the optical stations. In effect, there was no limit to the range of electrical cables. In principle at least, they could span the Atlantic or even encircle the world.

However, if a global network of cables existed, then any ship could sail into virtually any port in the world and could be connected instantly to the rest of the world. Unknown to Edward, at the time, a global network of electrical cables eventually became a reality in less than a century. Shortly after, it was radio transmission, that finally solved the last remaining problem of ship-to-ship and ship-to-shore communications.

None of this was particularly good news from the Admiralty's point of view, although Edward had identified the immediate objectives and where the effort should be concentrated. His principal task now, was to put his thoughts on paper. How he wished that he could consult Sybil, moreover, her handwriting was neater and more consistent than his.

Friday, 31 January 1817
Letter from Jerry says my reports arrived. FNL very appreciative f my efforts. Noted my concerns about code books.

Reminded me to send in my claim for expenses. Asked me to submit plan for extended route Devonport to Falmouth.

By the end of the month, Edward had completed all three reports for the First Naval Lord, written in his own fair hand. The reports were immediately delivered by hand to the Admiralty. The following day he received a note from Jerry who passed on his Lordship's appreciation for all his efforts, and thanked Edward for his candid observations about the careless way that code books were kept so insecurely. His note also reminded Edward to submit an account of his expenses. His Lordship also requested that Edward should prepare a plan to extend his optical cable beyond Devonport to Falmouth.

Monday 3 February 1817
Prepared list of repeater stations Falmouth to Devonport
Falmouth to Truro (11 miles)
Grampound (10 miles)
St Austell (6 miles)
Fowey (8 miles)
Looe (10 miles)
St Germans (8 miles)
Devonport (10 miles)
Portsmouth to Devonport is suspended at present.
Proposed locations for optical cable stations.
Portsdown Hill to Wickham (6 miles)
Eastliegh (11 miles)
Totton (10 miles)
Bramshaw (9 miles)

Fordingbrdge (9 miles)
Cranborne (7 miles)
Tarrant Hinton (12 Miles)
Blandford (6 miles)
Milborne St Andrews (9 miles)
Dorchester (9 miles)
Winterborne (6 miles)
Bridport (10 miles)
Lyme Regis (10 miles)
Seaton (8 miles)
Newton Poppleford (10 miles)
Exminster (11 miles)
Dawlish (9 miles)
Newton Abbot (10 miles)
Totnes (8 miles)
South Brent (9 miles)
Ivybridge (7 miles)
Plympton (7 miles)
Devonport docks (7 miles)
Some stations are very remote. May need sleeping quarters.

With the aid of local maps, Edward quickly devised a route of six extra repeater stations between Devonport and Falmouth. The notebook lists these extra stations and the cable lengths as:
Falmouth to Truro (11 miles)
Grampound (10 miles)
St Austell (6 miles)
Fowey (8 miles)
Looe (10 miles)
St Germans (8 miles)

Devonport (10 miles)

Edward proposed using anonymous rented shop premises for his repeater stations.

The Devonport line itself, was an extension of the Portsmouth line. Since the Devonport extension had been suspended, Edward didn't feel constrained to use any of the planned semaphore stations. The repeater stations he listed were:

Portsdown Hill to Wickham (6 miles)
Eastliegh (11 miles)
Totton (10 miles)
Bramshaw (9 miles)
Fordingbrdge (9 miles)
Cranborne (7 miles)
Tarrant Hinton (12 Miles)
Blandford (6 miles)
Milborne St Andrews (9 miles)
Dorchester (9 miles)
Winterborne (6 miles)
Bridport (10 miles)
Lyme Regis (10 miles)
Seaton (8 miles)
Newton Poppleford (10 miles)
Exminster (11 miles)
Dawlish (9 miles)
Newton Abbot (10 miles)
Totnes (8 miles)
South Brent (9 miles)
Ivybridge (7 miles)

Plympton (7 miles)

Devonport docks (7 miles)

This was a very long line, so Edward was not surprised that the line was suspended. The line was 202 miles long and required 102 bobbins of 2-mile cable.

Monday, 10 February 1817

Portsmouth line currently under construction.

Proposed changes for optical cable route.

Delete Chelsea

Delete Putney Heath

Kennington to Kingston Thames (10 miles)

Change Esher to Weybridge (9 miles)

Woking (8 miles)

Guildford (7 miles)

Change Godalming to Milford Whitley (10 miles)

Haslemere (6 miles)

Midhurst (9 miles)

South Harting (8 miles)

Change Compton Down to Rowlands Castle (8 miles)

Portsdown Hill (9 miles)

Delete Lumps Fort

Portsmouth dockyards (8 miles)

Proposed changes to Chatham line beyond Shooters Hill.

Dartford (8 miles)

Gravesend (7 miles)

Chatham docks (9 miles).

The notebook also lists some small changes to the London to Portsmouth cable which reduced the number of stations by three:
Delete Chelsea
Delete Putney Heath
Kennington to Kingston Thames (10 miles)
Change Esher to Weybridge (9 miles)
Woking (8 miles)
Guildford (7 miles)
Change Godalming to Milford Whitley (10 miles)
Haslemere (6 miles)
Midhurst (9 miles)
South Harting (8 miles)
Change Compton Down to Rowlands Castle (8 miles)
Portsdown Hill (9 miles)
Delete Lumps Fort
Portsmouth dockyards (8 miles)
The reason for these changes was that some of the original planned stations were more than 10 miles apart.

At that time there were no routes between big cities administered by a single Turnpike Trust. Most routes had countless small Trusts controlling small sections of the route. Like the route to Chatham, Edward planned to run his cables on posts alongside the turnpikes. If permits were required, then it was the responsibility of the Admiralty to arrange this.

In the case of the Chatham line, there were too many proposed stations and they were at the wrong intervals. From Shooters Hill he proposed stations at:

Dartford (8 miles)

Gravesend (7 miles)

Chatham docks (9 miles).

Edward didn't need the stations at Swanscombe, Gads Hill, Callum Hill, or Beacon Hill. His proposal was far more direct and used fewer stations. In the notebook he suggests using rented shop or commercial premises instead of the Admiralty built semaphore stations.

Edward knew precisely what his strengths were; he was an engineer, specialising in mechanisms, whereas people like Michael Faraday were experimental scientists. He was not able to compete with such people, in terms of investigating very bright light sources. Edward already knew about 'Arch' light (carbon electrode arc light), but this needed an electrical source of energy that was not available at that time. The best that he could do was harness the sun, whenever it was available. He knew that a very simple coupling could be made between incoming and outgoing cables at repeater stations, to adapt them to much brighter light sources, should they become available in the future. Indeed, such a light did become available within a few years. Limelight, was capable of transmission beyond 50 miles, but it depended on oxygen gas, which at that time was not in commercial production. In all other respects, limelight would have been the perfect solution.

Tuesday, 18 February 1817
New idea. Use lenses to focus light to a point. Must be much brighter. Tried candle flame with success. Also tried rotating mirror. Clockwork? Any other method. Decided mirror not needed. Make focus larger. Approx 0.07 inch. Modify Argand lamp.

Edward did have one idea of his own that he intended to pursue. His opinion was that the brightness of a lamp flame could be focused with lenses to produce a very bright point of light. If this point was shared amongst the six filaments by quickly rotating this point with mirrors, then this must be an improvement. He did a provisional experiment with a candle flame and a rotating hexagonal mirror and was amazed to find that at 24 revolutions per second the flame appeared to be static and constant. Further experiments with a microscope lens revealed that the point source of light appeared to be at least ten times brighter and possibly more. At a stroke he had improved the reliability of his cable, although he admitted that he still had the problem of rotating the mirror at 24 revolutions per second, day and night. The notebook had an annotation (Clockwork? Any other way). On reflection, Edward concluded that a rotating mirror was not the answer. If the focus point of the light was approximately 0.07-inches diameter, then all six filaments could be packed into this zone without mirrors. The notebook also has another comment, (Argand lamps). I assume that this was a reminder to design such a lamp, probably based on something that was already available at a reasonable price, that could be adapted to accept a powerful lens and six filaments.

Edward already had the bones of an idea for 'scrambling' messages prior to coding, but this involved a moderately large device to mechanically remember a 100-letter message and then to re-arrange it. He could produce such a device, this instant, but it wouldn't be very elegant. He was satisfied that his current coding arrangements were sufficient, apart from the Admiralty reliance on code books. He was also confident that his paper tapes were an ideal way to carry coded messages around the various Navy establishments without the contents being the revealed to anybody. He had already demonstrated, during the Chatham test, how easy it was to train suitable operators.

Thursday, 20 February 1817
Scrambling messages. Idea will not leave my mind alone. Crude device of composing stick (wooden channel) containing message written on wooden beads. Devide stick into say 4 parts. Mount short sticks side by side and scrape off bottom row of beads onto scramble stick. Keep repeating. Second thoughts – why bother? Use this method to create code disks. Asked cabinet makers to produce working model. Played with model with (S). Found second pass unscrambles code. Better still turn short sticks up-side-down. (S) astonished. Thought about ivory beads

but too expensive. Toyed with creating oriental script for private matters . Utterly inscrutable but draws attention to text. Not worth the effort.

Despite all the other matters that Edward had to content with, the idea of scrambling messages would not go away. In the end one morning, while he was nursing a cup of tea, he confronted the problem again and sketched his rather cumbersome idea of a 'composing' stick where the original message could be set out with wooden beads with painted letters of the alphabet. This stick could be separated into several short lengths all stacked together, side by side. A simple lug driven by a clockwork engine could then scrape away the bottom row of beads and deposit them onto a second, long 'composing' stick. Obviously, the new order of the letters in the message would be scrambled. It was certainly simple and workable, but it was definitely not elegant.

Suddenly it dawned on him that he had inadvertently devised a way to scramble the letters on a code disc. Why bother to provide a separate scrambling method for the Admiralty, when it could be incorporated in the current code disc. He now had a method of generating an infinite variety of random code discs, depending on the length of the short parts of the long composing stick. He made some annotations on his sketch and handed it to the foreman cabinet maker.

The following day, in the company of Sybil, he played with his new toy, using the 31 characters from a coding machine. It was while he played with the device, that he discovered the trick of assembling the short sticks upside-down. This made sure that the first letter of the scrambled order was always different. He also discovered that if he ran his device a second time, starting with a scrambled stick, it would restore the original order. The problem was solved, and the job was done. Sybil shook her head in disbelief that anybody could have such a cunning mind. She just accepted the fact that it was now her job to keep a record of how the numbered code discs were originally constructed in case they had to make replacements. Edward even contemplated using Tagua nuts (vegetable ivory) instead of wooden beads but decided that this was an unnecessary extravagance.

Edward did toy with the idea of writing about private matters in the Notebook in an oriental script, but decided against it because it only drew attention to the private matters. He notes that the Chinese or Japanese characters were utterly inscrutable. There are no examples for us to judge

CABLE MAKING

Monday, 3 March 1817
Order for Chatham line arrived for cable and equipment.
24 working starts. Hired extra hands and glassman. Target two ten-mile cables per month. One 2-mile section every 3 days. Meet foremen every Monday to review targets. Workshop moves into urgent mode. V. excited. At last meeting with FNL he agreed to anonymous shop premises as long as not directly connected with Admiralty. Fix brass plate A & C. (S) will recruit and train staff with help from Sally – Jimmy's wife. Estimate premises will come in service 24 hours from connection. FNL likes speed of connection. Much improved on semaphore stations. Terminus station must always be Navy premises (semaphore station). Jimmy self promoted to transport manager. Carters not always literate so they use tavern names. (S) as always has target of being paid on time.
Also order for Portsmouth cable.

The order finally came through from the Admiralty to complete the optical cable from Kennington to Chatham, complete with all necessary items for coding and de-coding messages at both ends, as well as repeating equipment at intermediate stations.

That very same day Sybil wrote out a whole series of invoices in the most minute detail, ready to be issued the moment each item was delivered. For his part Edward toured the workshop to warn the workers that day and night filament production would commence the following day. The modified production process was now capable of producing two filaments of 2-miles length every 12 hours. The target was one 2-mile cable of 12 filaments every 3 days at 24 hours working. A ten-mile stretch would be delivered on site every fifteen days (two 10-mile lengths per month). Workers assigned to 24-hour tasks would work relays of 8-hours maximum but would be paid for 12 hours work. Extra hands (including an extra glassman) would be hired to ensure the production line was fully manned for all three shifts. The metalworkers would be expected to produce a minimum of four repeater station devices, and ten pairs of cable couplings per month and one coder or decoder machine every two months. The cabinet makers would be expected to produce mahogany cabinets for all the devices produced by the metalworkers and enough limewood bobbins to wind the cables onto. Edward would meet all the foremen every Monday morning to review whether these targets were being met. The notebook records that the workshop immediately took on a mood of urgency spurred on by the big increase in wages. Ayres and Compton had never seen anything like it before.

At a previous meeting with the First Naval Lord, Edward managed to persuade him that renting anonymous shop properties along the route of the cable provided a cheap and exceedingly quick way of achieving an almost instant repeater station. There would be no obvious link between these premises and the Admiralty. Indeed, it was Edward's intention that each shop premises would bear a brass plate engraved; Ayres, Compton and Raine, Leadenhall Street, London. Edward estimated that it would only take 24 hours to equip and connect a shop or rooms to the cable, and once connected the repeater station would become immediately operational. The rental costs would be partly offset by the lower female wages of the staff. It seems his Lordship was most persuaded by the speed that the optical cable would become serviceable. He also liked the idea of absolute anonymity and the fact that the female staff would have no idea what they were engaged in: they just looked at pretty lights and pressed buttons. The only stipulation was that the terminus at both ends of the cable had to be on Naval property. This approval resulted in the three stations along the Chatham line becoming operational within two months.

It was reliable Sybil, who recruited suitable young ladies at each station location. It was also she who vetted the rented properties to ensure they had suitable toilet facilities, and space to prepare and eat food and drink. Again, it was Sybil who also trained the young staff. Amazingly, she also managed to keep the company books up to date. None of these activities escaped the attention of Edward, who made sure she was appropriately compensated. She also suggested that they should open a training school close by, because there would soon be many more staff to train. It would be far more economical to do it all in one place rather than travelling across country. She even suggested that Sally, the boilerman's wife might want to help as a part-time instructor at the school.

In a matter of days, Sybil had requisitioned space in the next-door premises for a training room, and a day later the carpenters fitted partitions to enclose the room. Fortunately, the production of repeater boxes was ahead of schedule, so some were diverted to the training school, along with many spare, short lengths of cable to connect them together. Sybil acted as the sender and Sally acted as the receiver, while the trainees merely passed on the messages. Edward had to admit that Sybil had done a remarkable job. He also acknowledged that Sally took to the task as if she had been born to it. There is every reason to believe that Sally enjoyed her days out and the extra money, and that she blossomed in self-confidence, although the notebook makes no mention of this.

Sally's husband, Jimmy Welland, the boilerman, stoker and general handyman, also changed into a higher gear to become the self-styled transport manager. It was he who organized the continuous stream of carters to arrive at the backyard to take away the finished bobbins of cable and made sure that each carrier knew whereabouts on the cable route that they were heading for. Since most of the cart drivers were, at best, semi-literate Jimmy devised a map system based on Tavern names. Again, his efforts did not escape the watchful eye of Edward, who hired a strong young lad to take over the stoking and other duties that Jimmy normally performed. It was probably a matter of personal pride for Jimmy to remain the major bread-winner now that his wife was also working at the firm. When his children were old enough, Jimmy hoped that they too would join the firm. He was not the best educated man around, but at least he could recognize a good employer when he saw one.

Sybil, for her part kept an eagle eye on the accounts and constantly checked that production targets and delivery dates were being met. As far as the Admiralty was concerned Edward's firm were the epitome of reliability. Amazingly, Sybil even managed to get paid on time by the Admiralty, although I suspect that this had more to do with the fact that the optical telegraph was a pet project of his Lordship.

Friday, 2 May 1817
Meeting with FNL. Chatham order completed and working.
FNL not in good mood. Portsmouth line still in construction.
Wants to call a halt, but Contract dept urge caution. FNL
gives us order to lay cable and open premises to Portsmouth.
Expects completion in six months. V angry so he cancelled the
whole of the Devonport extension. No longer suspended – now
cancelled. Looks like we will get Devonport order too, in time.
Suggested Devonport requires no investment in building
stations. Also suggested cable itself could be supplied under
'maintenance contract' again no capital cost. FNL accepted

proposal. Job done. Order for Devonport in hand. Expected completion 12 months after Portsmouth contract (very long line) more than 200 miles.

Following the completion of the Chatham line, The First Naval Lord gave Edward permission to lay the cable to Portsmouth, using shop premises, long before the buildings had been finished on the new semaphore line. He expected Edward to complete the line in six months. At one of the regular meetings with the First Naval Lord, his lordship was fuming at the slow progress of the semaphore line and wanted done with it all. He probably would have scrapped the whole line there and then, had it not been for the intervention of the Contracts Branch who pointed out that the Admiralty would be faced with expensive contractual problems. It would be cheaper to just finish the job, even if it wasn't used. Fortunately, no contracts had yet been awarded for the Devonport extension, so his Lordship vented his anger by cancelling the whole of that semaphore extension.

Edward, prudently decided to wait for the anger to subside before raising the issue of continuing cable production for the Devonport line. He later pointed out to his lordship that renting premises required no capital investment in the Devonport line. He was also prepared to supply the cable for this line under a maintenance contract that would cover the premises rentals too. In effect his lordship would be getting the Devonport extension at no immediate cost. It was a very tempting offer, which his lordship accepted.

Edward warned Sybil of the slight change in payment rules for the Devonport line, but at least they had guaranteed and profitable work for the next twelve months alone. Sybil suggested temporarily moving the training school to a more central location, such as Lyme Regis, rather than asking the female staff to travel all the way to London. In the end she later decided to hold three training sessions at Fordingbridge, Lyme Regis and Newton Abbot.

Wednesday, 12 November 1817
Portsmouth contract completed. Line to Portsmouth open and working. New 'signals room open at Admiralty. FNL agreed all officers would be issued with Identity number (part of header code), so we know who to deliver the message to. Mood at Admiralty V. relaxed – no wars! (S) says Navy is probably under-manning semaphore line to save money. (S) thinks Navy has budget problems. Production line carries on to Devonport. 200 miles of cable to lay. Six station extension to Falmouth approved. A big surprise. Took (E) on travelling holiday to west country looking for premises. Loved the countryside and people. (S) thinks training should be done locally – too far to travel to London. (S) asked about pay rates. Country rate is much less than London rate. Not my problem. Admiralty are paying.

Meanwhile a 'Signals' room had been set aside at the Admiralty, for the optical cable traffic, now that Chatham and Portsmouth were both fully functioning.

Apart from a few minor teething problems, both lines settled down to a steady routine. One of the initial problems concerned how to address messages to specific persons. Eventually the Admiralty agreed that all officers at all locations would be assigned a personal Identity Number, which appeared on the header line of all messages immediately after the code disc number.

In the absence of any further threat from an invasion from France or any hostile actions from America after the Treaty of Ghent, the pressure on the Admiralty was off. In these circumstances it was normal for the Admiralty to cease spending, so it came as a surprise that Edward was given permission to complete the six-station extension from Devonport all the way to Falmouth, although the firm was asked to submit six separate invoices as and when each station was completed. It was Sybil's opinion that the Admiralty were attempting to conceal the contract, as a whole, by splitting it into very small parts that could be more easily 'lost' within the overall budget.

It was Sybil's view that probably the whole cable venture was financed by under-the-table transactions. It was her view that Admiralty accounts showed a deficit that couldn't reasonably be explained, which was more than likely the real reason that the Devonport extension was abandoned. There was no possible way that the Admiralty could justify the cost of sending dispatches to London from Falmouth, by riders, let alone the waste of time.

In view of the very few messages sent by the real semaphore, Sybil suggested that the Admiralty were under-manning the semaphore stations, or only working part time to fund the optical cable. Provided the Admiralty communications were working and provided it didn't cost any more than the original estimates, then the Public Auditors would be satisfied. Even the shop premises rentals and operator's wages were charged as 'maintenance fees' to the Admiralty

It took almost a year to make the 102 2-mile bobbins for the Devonport line. As fast as the cable was being made, Jimmy and his band of carters were transporting the bobbins to their locations.

Previously Edward had taken Elsie on a two-week travelling holiday along the Devonport route, to find suitable premises and to hire local contractors to erect the posts and support wire for his cable. Elsie was captivated by the Dorset and Devon countryside. Edward was captivated by Elsie and was exhausted at the end of two weeks.

On his return, Sybil took Edward's list of premises and confirmed the rental agreements. It was now her turn to take a tour of the 'West Country' to recruit young ladies as operators. The cost of the rentals was so much lower than London rentals, that Sybil decided to use the premises as temporary safe storage for the bobbins. She also decided that the first ten stations up to Blandford should be occupied by female staff immediately. In this way, the moment the cable was laid to a repeater station, it could begin operations instantly. She also took addresses from all the applicants so that she could contact them when they would be required later in the year.

On her return, Sybil commented to Edward that the firm was paying all the female staff the same rate regardless of their location. Wage rates for women in the countryside were considerably less than the London rate. Edward pointed out that there was no justification for paying women 'slave' wages. The admiralty was already getting cheap labour, so they were not complaining, and neither was Edward complaining. If it turns out that his staff in the countryside were being relatively well paid, then good for them. Sybil just smiled.

Jimmy was rightly proud that his band of carters delivered their loads of bobbins on time. The local contractors laying the posts and wire supports were not always on time, but a sharp reminder from the foreman cable layer usually meant that they were rarely more than a day late. Surprisingly, there was no shortage of volunteers for the cable laying team, probably because it was a holiday in very pleasant surroundings.

151

Friday, 11 September 1818
Line to Devonport completed and working. Felt very proud.
Congratulated workshop on job well done. Only falmouth
extension to comple. Probably next 3 months. FNL very happy
with astonishing progress. I want regular reports from all
repeater stations. Will take (E) on holiday again for two weeks.
Then stop cable production. Should have few spare bobbins for
repairs.

In all, it took ten months to complete the line to Devonport, with repeater stations coming on line every three days. Edward felt very proud of his workers every time he reported progress to his lordship.

Within the next three months the Falmouth extension was complete and linked to the terminus at Devonport for onwards transmission to Portsmouth, rather than a direct line to London. On the surface, it appears that the Admiralty had achieved their objective, without paying for it. The cable production line was run for a further two weeks to build up a stock of reserve bobbins for repairs and accidents.

At Sybil's suggestion, Edward made plans to visit every single repeater station to gather comments from the operators, and to arrange for them to send in weekly reports by mail, addressed to him personally at work. Edward wanted to be ahead of the game in case anything was about to go wrong. He particularly wanted regular reports of the brightness levels of the signals.

It was again a sort of travelling holiday for Elsie and himself and took just over two weeks to complete. Edward found that the presence of Elsie helped to put the operators at ease, and more willing to be candid in their comments. On Edward's return, the filament production line was shut down and life returned to normal in the workshop.

Monday, 4 January 1819
Falmouth extension completed and working.
Weekly reports arrive from all stations. Light brightness always good to very good. Several complaints about filling oil lamps. Must devise a better method – less messy, non spill. Give the task to metal workers. (E) suggests ceramic dish to collect smoke and add fragrance to air. Good idea. No complaits from Admiralty. Counted messages each moth. Portsmouth biggest user. Next Chatham. Very few from Falmouth. Least from Devonport. Night time usage almost nil. I need access to repeater station operators. Devised Identity Code numbers. Don't think Admiralty will agree to codes/de-codes. Perhaps train operators to use uncoded messages. Nothing to hide. Wait for FNL good mood.

The performance reports arrived on Edward's desk with monotonous regularity. Without exception, the operators reported the signal brightness as good to very good, largely depending on the interval distance between repeater stations. Periodically, the operators were interrupted by the public, asking whether they could arrange for instruments, made by Ayres and

Compton, to be repaired. The operators had been pre-warned to re-direct such enquiries to the Leadenhall Street branch. The most frequent complaint concerned the Argand lamps, or more precisely re-filling these lamps with Colza oil. Apparently, it was messy and prone to spillage or over filling.

Edward put his inventive mind to devising a solution, a long spout, non-spill can or jug. He invited Elsie to try out several designs, and it was from Elsie that he picked up a tip to put a shallow ceramic dish over the glass funnel to collect the soot particles. In fact, Elsie also filled the dish with scented oils to perfume the atmosphere. She also told Edward that she cleaned the dishes weekly with alcohol to remove the soot and perfume residues. Edward immediately contacted an agent for a Staffordshire pottery to manufacture these dishes, standing on three little feet, to allow space for the air to flow freely from the glass funnel. In the meantime, the metalworkers were assigned the task of making the brass cans with long thin spouts. In a matter of weeks there were enough boxed kits for each repeater station, with a sheet of printed instructions (written by Sybil). These were dispatched by Jimmy to all the repeater stations.

As expected, the incoming weekly reports came in with very positive messages about the beautiful new filling cans and the wonderful aroma dishes. The signal brightness reports continued to be very good. As far as the repeater stations were concerned, the whole network appeared to be functioning well. There were no complaints from Jerry, so it seemed that the coding and decoding machines were also doing their job.

On his monthly visits to the Admiralty, Edward always counted the number of messages received, just to get a feel for who was using the telegraph most. The biggest user by far was Portsmouth, followed by Chatham, and then a long way behind was Falmouth and finally Devonport. It was interesting to note that the night time service was hardly ever used. Edward was not surprised, because the country was not currently at war with anyone. Apparently, the Admiralty decided that a daily 9:00 am message should be sent to all terminals announcing Greenwich time, which Edward fully approved of.

Edward found it irksome that he personally couldn't use his optical telegraph to send messages to any of his operators directly. He had already worked out a method of using special Identity Numbers to contact each repeater station, and of course he could use un-coded messages. However, his staff would still need a decoding machine to read coded messages. He was certain that his Lordship would not approve of decoding machines in the hands of amateurs or non-Navy persons. The problem would have to remain irksome. On the other hand, the operators could always translate un-coded signals manually, letter by letter (i.e. code

155

disc signature 000). He would have to wait for his Lordship to be in a very good mood before he broached the subject.

Thursday, 10 February 1820
Meeting with FNL at Admiralty. Every station running smoothly. Sir Graham Moore will depart in March. Thanked me for my efforts. Wished me well for future. Jerry asked me to put in good word. I suggested Jerry should be in charge of Signals room. FNL agreed. Successor, Sir William Hope is man of poor health. I do not expect same degree of help and support as Sir Graham so FNL suggested all future meetings and contact should be with Lieutenant Ballard.
Still need to contact my operators. Could tap into Kennington cable. (S) and (E) say no- too risky. Jerry agreed to intercept these messages and to bring them to me direct.

Just prior to Sir Graham Moore's departure from the board of the Admiralty in March 1820, he summoned Edward to his office, to thank him for his efforts to establish the optical telegraph, and to praise its flawless performance. While his Lordship was in such a good mood, Edward asked if Lieutenant Ballard could be rewarded in some measure for his contribution to this success. Perhaps he could be promoted in charge of 'Signals'. In this case Edward could report directly to Jerry rather than the new incoming First Naval Lord, Sir William Hope. Subsequently, Jerry was elevated to Officer in charge of Signals, which was just as well, because Sir William Hope was not a man of good health and barely made any decisions during his tenure as First Naval Lord until his departure in May 1827. He was succeeded by Sir George Cockburn in September 1828. Following the departure of Sir Graham Moore, Edward had no further orders to report to the First Naval Lord, instead he was instructed to report to Lieutenant Ballard.

This change of the chain of command worked very much in Edward's favour. Initially, Edward was approached by Jerry, to put in a good word for him with Sir Graham before his departure, because he knew that Sir Graham held Edward in very high esteem. Edward did his part and in return Jerry did his part by being most co-operative.

The idea of being able to communicate with all the repeater station operators had nagged his brain ever since he got the idea. At one time he even contemplated secretly tapping into the Kennington terminus, where all the incoming cables converged before being passed on to the Admiralty. Both Elsie and Sybil considered the idea was dangerous and foolhardy. Why endanger his career for so little reward? How often had an emergency arisen since the telegraph had been installed?

Now that Jerry was fully onboard and owed Edward a favour, Edward tried an alternative way of contacting the operators. Edward was quite happy to use un-coded messages to his operators, because he had nothing to

157

hide. These messages would be preceded by a message signature '000' for the code disc. This was a simple way to recognize these non-Navy messages. Edward asked Jerry to train his operators to intercept these messages and retain them for the attention of himself, rather than transmit them onwards to Whitehall. The Navy operators were free to read these messages, and if they contained the word 'urgent' then a rider should be dispatched to take the message to Edward at his office or at home in Norwood. Clearly nothing under-hand was going on, so Jerry readily agreed. Edward had achieved his objective and could use the Kennington repeater station for sending and receiving messages to and from his operators. Most importantly, Kennington was manned around the clock, so urgent messages would be acted on almost immediately.

Some eight years later, this tiny change in the telegraph procedures bore fruit.

THE PROPOSITION

Extracts from the Optics Notebook (private matters)

Monday, 15 February 1819
(M) and child thrown out. (E) v. upset.
Friday, 19 February 1819
(M) and (E) sisters. Child Peter – father, soldier killed.
Suggested (M) moves to farmhouse. (E) delighted.
Monday, 22 February 1819
(E) childless. (M) suggests having child for (E) in gratitude. I agree.
Monday ,1 March 1819
Second thoughts. Will new child change (E)? Not enthusiastic. Reluctant but under pressure.
Thursday, 4 March 1819
Started process with (M). V. awkward. (M) asked my middle name. Had to admit it was Brendan. My mother's father was Irish. I detest the name myself but (M) says it is poetic. Must admit (M) v. pretty. Good influence on (E) hair/dress/etc.
Thursday ,15 April 1819
Success with (M). (E) very grateful. Exhausted. Confirmed with doctor (M) pretends to be (E).
Wednesday, 12 January 1820
Birth of Amy. Mother and child well. (E) delighted.
Tuesday, 6 June 1820
(E) and (M) miss mother. Suggest plan to bring her to farmhouse. Meet at grocers F & T at LL eDul. Much kissing. Too much from (M).
Saturday ,10 June 1820

Met (F) at grocers. Asks too many questions. Delighted to see (E) and (M) and children. V. happy day for all. Invited (F) to visit weekly. Calls me Capt. Edwards. Asked who my wife was because I treat (E) and (M) so kindly. Asked her who she thought. (F) says (E). No need to confess the truth.

The Optics Notebook was primarily a notebook concerned with Edward's work, and rarely referred to private or domestic issues, except for sparse, cryptic notes, limited to one or two words at best. Attempting to combine these periodic references together into a coherent narrative is well nigh impossible, so a degree of imagination is required to make any sense of these jottings.

There are a host of other events that occurred in the world beyond Edward's work and small domestic issues, but for the most part the Optics Notebook ignores them all. There is no mention of Queen Victoria's coronation in 1837, nor the introduction of the Penny Post in 1840, nor the Cholera epidemic of 1849, nor the Great Exhibition in 1851, and not even the fact that so many Navy ships were at sea in 1851 (129) that only 35 were left to defend the nation. Even the break in the trans-Atlantic telegraph cable in 1858 escaped a mention in the Notebook.

There is a strange, single line comment in the notebook (M & child thrown out). It later transpires from more little snippets, that Mary was the sister of Elsie. Mary had given birth to an illegitimate child, Peter, whose father had been killed in action in the Army. It seems that Mary's father disapproved of her and the child and in a fit of anger, evicted them from his house. Elsie was devastated, until Edward offered to take them in at the farmhouse.

It seems that when Edward and Elsie rescued her sister Mary and her baby from the pit of poverty and degradation, Mary was profoundly and eternally grateful. She seamlessly joined the household and instantly became part of their family. Edward notes that Mary is very pretty and is a good influence on Elsie with respect to her appearance. Mary probably persuaded Elsie to change her hair style (no more tight bun at the back) and advised her to modernise her dresses. It is likely that they began to look more like real sisters (or even twins). Baby Peter brought out Edward's fatherly instincts and aroused Elsie's motherly instincts. It appears that Elsie was unable to bear children, so out of gratitude Mary offered to bear another child for her sister. For Elsie, this was the nearest thing to a child of her own and was suitably grateful and supportive of Mary's offer.

Initially, Edward too supported the idea, but his enthusiasm weakened when he realized what being the father of this child entailed. He was exceedingly reluctant to jeopardize his relationship with Elsie, even though they were not yet married. The idea of having a relationship with her sister seemed to him somehow immoral and sinful. Elsie took exactly the opposite view. If Mary had been a stranger, then it might have been a risky venture, but Mary was her sister, and that made all the difference and made it acceptable.

At first Edward refused, but eventually he was worn down by Elsie's persistence. Edward finally gave in and pacified his conscience with the thought that Elsie would ultimately achieve motherhood despite Nature's cruel legacy. Edward was already pretending to be two people, so perhaps his conscience could accept that he could love two women at the same time. We will never know.

Obviously, we cannot be sure what passed between Edward and Mary, but I would guess that it would have been an uphill struggle for Mary to get Edward to perform, not just the once, but every night until she knew for certain that she was pregnant. Elsie, for her part waited patiently, without complaint until Mary announced her good news. Elsie was ecstatic and couldn't wait to celebrate with Edward, who was probably completely drained by that time. Curiously Mary asked what Edward's middle name was. He admitted that it was Brendan (after his mother's father, who was Irish). Clearly Edward disliked the name but Mary thought it was poetic.

I think that it is fair to say that Edward's trust in Elsie was absolute, whereas reading between the lines, Edward was not so sure about Mary. Edward was cautious and watchful with respect to Mary, probably because he didn't want to do anything that might hurt Elsie's feelings, regardless of how innocent it might be. The Optics Notebook reveals that periodically Mary showed too much love and affection for Edward, but he was always on the alert and spotted the signs. How Edward managed to maintain this vigilance over the years and still keep the peace, is a mystery. The sword of Damoclese hung over Edward for many years, but he survived. Elsie's trust in Edward was also absolute. Suspicion was not a member of their household, which probably accounts for the peace lasting a lifetime.

Edward was at pains to explain to the girls that a simple charade would be necessary, where the girls would exchange identities for the benefit of the doctor and eventually for the midwife or nurses. Edward would play his part as the dutiful husband and Mary would play the part of his wife. Edward had the distinct impression that Mary was over-enthusiastic about the charade. Elsie was her patient self as usual. Whatever their motives, it seems the charade was successful.

In time, Mary went into labour and gave birth to a baby girl (Amy) and survived childbirth. Amy was bought up believing that Elsie was her mother and Peter was brought up believing that Mary was his mother. The two children were always treated equally as brother and sister. The whole family continued to live together in happiness and harmony for many years. Whilst many might say this was a peculiar arrangement, in some undisclosed way Edward, Elsie and Mary made the relationship work for them.

Edward overheard Elsie and Mary discussing their concern that their mother was not able to share the good news. Mary had been the victim of her father's irrational bad temper, but she was certain that her mother didn't share his views but was too frightened to object. Both she and Elsie were longing to see their mother again.

Without revealing his intentions, Edward discovered that Florence (their mother) and Tom (their father) lived in a modest house behind Lordship Lane in East Dulwich. We already know that Edward was very bright and very resourceful, so it didn't take him long to discover when and where Florence did her weekly shopping, just by following her.

We cannot be certain about these common names of the times, because the Notebook only refers to their initials, e.g. F & T at LL eDul.

Originally, he just intended to arrive on the farmhouse doorstep with 'Grandma' as a surprise guest, but this would have been unfair on the girls, because they would obviously want to tidy up and present themselves and the children in their 'Sunday best'. Edward relented and told the girls of his plan. The girls were overjoyed at the plan and showered Edward with kisses. The Notebook records that Mary's joy was too enthusiastic.

On the next shopping day, Edward took the day off and dressed in his Naval uniform, he drove his carriage to Goose Green to intercept Florence in the grocery shop. Just as Florence was about to pay for her groceries, Edward stepped forwards, introduced himself as Lieutenant Edward Raine and informed Florence that her birthday had arrive early this year, and that he would pay her bill as a present.

Florence raised her hand to her mouth in shock and surprise: too shocked to say a word. Edward announced that her carriage awaited outside to take her to Norwood, where another present awaited her. On the way to the farmhouse Florence eventually found her tongue as she questioned Edward about who he was and where they were going, and would it take a long time? She insisted on calling him Captain Edwards regardless of how many times he repeated his name. In his own affable way, Edward reassured her that they would soon arrive in Norwood, and that he knew she would be overjoyed at the present that awaited her.

As they entered the farmhouse, Elsie and Mary were there, with the children, to greet Florence. After the initial shock came floods of tears of happiness. Following the tears came a barrage of questions from the girls and from Florence herself. Edward gently urged them towards the dining room, where the girls had prepared a sumptuous lunch. Over lunch Florence had gathered her composure enough to admonish Edward for his wicked deceit but admitted that the 'present' had been the most wonderful gift that she could have hoped for.

Thereafter, Grandma became a regular visitor to the farmhouse. She did make one observation that Edward found slightly disturbing; that Edward treated both of her daughters with such kindness and generosity, that she wasn't sure which of them he was married to. At that time, he wasn't married to either of them (I assume), and he certainly wasn't going to admit that had made love to both. Edward brushed her remark to one side and changed the subject by asking Florence who she thought was the happiest daughter. Grandma reflected for a moment and named Elsie. Edward stretched his arms wide, with palms uppermost as if to say that Florence had answered her own question.

I find it strange that Edward never mentioned a marriage between Elsie and himself, despite their obvious love for each other. Perhaps they got married in secret, shortly after she became his house keeper, or on one of their frequent holidays. Perhaps Edward felt it was not an appropriate subject to mention in his

Notebook. We will never know. Perhaps Elsie was against the idea after Amy was born. At least the two children would have the same surname, Hopkins. At that time, children born out of wedlock bore a social stigma that exposed them to unkind scorn and derision. Neither of the girls wanted that for their children.

LEGACY

In the United Kingdom, the first census was taken in 1801. The Raine family were not included because they probably lived elsewhere and didn't move to Norwood until after the second census in 1811. It is quite possible that they missed the next census in 1821 because the cart track called Spring Lane, leading to their farmhouse, was probably not on the maps at the time. Besides, it is likely that Elsie and Mary would have been reluctant to have anybody poking around into their private matters.

It has to remembered that any form of official documentation didn't exist before the Act of Parliament in 1836, which became law a year later. Prior to that date the Parochial Registers Act of 1812 required that Parish records were kept of marriages, births and burials, but these didn't apply to everybody. According to some estimates, up to 15% of all births were never recorded. The Births and Deaths Act of 1874 cured this anomaly by making the records compulsory. Even so, still-born children were not registered until 1924. The Marriages Act of 1836 allowed marriages by licence in approved premises, other than by Church of England clergy. I don't believe that Edward purposely evaded the paper trail, but clearly it was relatively easy to slip through the net. Little wonder that Edward, the girls, and their children have left so little documented evidence of their lives. It was as late as 1845 that the cause of death required certification by a doctor before a death certificate could be issued.

We know from the Optics Notebook that Edward survived at least until 1859 because he was present when Ayres and Compton shut their doors for the last time, and he made a final entry at home in 1859. What happened after that is anybody's guess. At that time, Peter and Amy would have been close to 40 years old. Certainly old enough to be married, with children of their own. The fact that Edward doesn't mention the children tells me that they probably were married and living elsewhere.

This was the age of affordable Rail travel, so Edward and the girls, could have moved to other parts of the kingdom, or they could have emigrated anywhere in the huge British Empire. Personally, the final entry in the Notebook suggests that Edward probably retired to the Dorset or Devon countryside, which Elsie loved so much. What happened to them? I don't suppose we will ever know.

The issue of documentary evidence is further complicated by Edward's work at the Admiralty, and the fact that he had a false persona that he could use whenever he wished. The secret nature of Edward's work didn't always work in his favour. I think it is very likely that Edward's collection of optical telegraph equipment never reached a museum is probably because the Admiralty objected, even though the equipment was out of date. It would have been very unlike the Admiralty to exhibit, for all to see, what they had been up for the past 30 years. They had managed to keep Edward and his activities secret and safe for all that time. More than likely, younger men with inscrutable minds had been recruited in the meantime. Why give it all away to their enemies (they had plenty) for the sake of a few dusty museum exhibits? Later, an accidental bombing raid in World War II resolved this problem forever.

During that same war, St Lukes church in Norwood was hit and the cemetary was also seriously damaged. The arrival of a railway station at West Norwood (originally called Lower Norwood) in 1856, was followed by heavy building developments over the whole area, including the two farm properties. On or around the time that Edward retired, he had already sold his farm property, or was in the process of doing so. He and his family moved elsewhere, leaving no trace of its existence.

I think the Optics Notebook gives us a fair glimpse of what Edward was like as a person; in his work he was hard working, fair, single-minded and something of a genius and in his domestic life he was responsible, loving and caring towards the two sisters and their children, even if the household arrangements were a little unconventional.

Based on what we do know about Edward and his family, could we reasonably speculate further about what happened next?

Firstly, although Norwood at the time was rural rather than urban, Edward had spent his life working in London, which was the largest city in the world at that time, and certainly the most heavily industrialised. With industrialisation came pollution, dirt and grime, which persisted for another century.

Fortunately for Edward and his family, they drank clean spring water, so they were not exposed to killers like cholera and typhoid fever, and the air was cleaner than the city itself, so they were at much less risk of tuberculosis and other lung diseases, except for Edward himself. It is highly likely that Edward suffered from mild dyspnoea (shortness of breath) at least, and probably other age related complaints too, such as loss of hearing, problems with vision and possibly diabetes.

What Edward needed most was a change of air: he needed to move out of the city. By this time the railway network had brought everywhere within easy reach of the urban centres, so there was no reason to stay inside the range of the mail coach. The coast or the countryside were all within a few hours by train. We know too, that Elsie loved the 'west country' from her trips to Dorset and Devon, so my guess is that the family moved to that area and most likely the seaside, because sea air was considered therapeutic at that time. Somewhere like Bournemouth, Weymouth, Lyme Regis, Torquay or Paignton would all have been suitable.

Edward was not exactly short of money, so I can well image that he would have bought the family a 'gentleman's residence' in any of these locations. It would have been healthy, comfortable and most of all anonymous. It would have been the ideal location for a respectable, wealthy family from the 'big city'. Probably the garden would have been as large as Edward's small holding in Norwood, and no doubt a local farm would have supplied milk daily. I can imagine that Edward would have installed a pure water supply from a spring or well. Gas for cooking and lighting would almost certainly have been available by that time. I can also imagine that Edward would have a little workshop in a shed somewhere in the garden to tinker with ideas and to repair household objects. I could guarantee that he had a microscope, a telescope, a box of assorted lens, a box of clockwork motors, and his trusty box of bench posts and clamps, not to mention a cylindrical slide rule. I think an anvil and potable forge were also close to hand. There would have been nothing that Edward couldn't make or repair.

What does Edward do now? For a short while he would tinker with household matters making sure that windows and doors opened and closed properly, and that water taps (fawcets) didn't drip and the drains were clear. Of course he would have written to Sybil, Jimmy, Sally and Jerry too. It is also likely that he invited them all to visit him in his 'mansion', as well as Grandma Florence, although in her case he probably invited her to stay for a week or more. These are the sort of things that we all do.

We have to keep in mind that Edward had spent a life time challenging his inventive brain on a daily basis. He is not going to sit idly doing nothing. Realistically, he is going to focus in on some aspect of life that triggers his attention and his ingenuity. He would be looking for better and smarter ways to do things, just as he had always done. Leopards do not change their spots. He would continue to read the newspapers to keep up to date, and he could afford to take a railway excursion to the British Museum or any other library for more detail.

Apart from his early apprenticeship, most of what Edward knew, came from his wide reading, and there is no reason why this would not continue. There is no indication that his brain had ceased to function. Age tends to slow down our ability to recognize and adapt to new ideas and concepts, but then skill and experience kicks in, which allows us to catch up with younger folk who may have been quicker off the mark.

Edward's knowledge of languages was probably limited, because he lived in the age of 'The British Empire', where English was the new 'lingua franca'. He had some knowledge of Latin, but it is doubtful that could read or understand Isaac Newton's 'Principia'. On the other hand he had probably read the English translation. He almost certainly had scant knowledge of French, Spanish or even German. He may have picked up a few words of Italian from his glass-workers. There would have been no pressure on the children to learn other languages. I doubt if there was any pressure or desire by Edward to travel abroad, so it is unlikely that he even contemplated emigration.

No doubt he would have found good schools for the children to attend, or he could afford to pay for private tutors. None of this stretches the imagination or is beyond probability. I think we can take it for granted that both Peter and Amy were very well educated. Edward would have certainly supported their education and I can believe that Elsie and Mary would have backed him up completely. At the time, education was considered the pathway to the future. I think that Edward would have been very eager to see both of the children attending university. There is no mention that the children were married but statistically there was a good chance that they were by the time Edward retired. His final Notebook comment was that they were happy and secure.

A very large proportion of the general population at that time were employed in domestic service, although I doubt if the household had any servants. Both Elsie and Mary knew all about hard work because they had both been 'in service'. Between the two girls, I believe that they were more than capable of running the household, although if they had guests, they may have had the help of local 'maids'.

The Notebook makes no mention of any social pursuits, either by Edward or the girls. There is no mention of the children having musical talents either, although we do have a reference that Edward liked brass band music and piano recitals, but not choral works. I think it is safe to say that in his retirement, Edward would not have had much interest in sporting activities or clubs, although if he was living near the sea, then one of his friends or acquaintances may have had a sailing boat, in which case, Edward would have made a good navigator, because he knew how to use a sextant. Indeed, he knew how to make one. If musicians or performers were visiting close to where Edward was living then I can imagine that he and the girls would have attended. In general, I would have said that the family kept very much to themselves in quiet respectability.

I suspect that what Edward craved for was intellectual stimulation, which would have been hard to come by in a quiet seaside setting, far from the busy hives of industry. The pages of history are littered with examples of people who contributed to the enlightenment of mankind, who lived far from big cities, but in Edward's case he thrived on improving the machines and the processes of industry to work better. Those machines are not usually found in rural settings. Edward was no longer surrounded on all sides by any evidence of innovation and progress. Even so, a genius of Edward's calibre would not have been deterred.

In fact the tone of his final Notebook entry is decidedly positive, with no regrets. He mentions a feeling of immense relief, and that he is looking forwards to starting all over again. The sense of relief may been because finally all his responsibilities and burdens had been lifted from his shoulders. The business was shut down, the optical telegraph had been dismantled, the children were off his hands (presumably married). All that remained were the charming and faithful sisters, Elsie and Mary. What more could he possibly want?

I am sure that Edward would have looked forward to periodic visits from Jerry Ballard, where they would have probably discussed the new steam propelled iron-clad ships of the day. I would bet that Edward was still looking for an application for his tiny compressed air engines that he developed for the filament process, now gently gathering dust in a Kennington warehouse.

We know that Edward was a skilled draughtsman, and we know that he often made sketches that his workmen could easily understand, which suggests to me that he was a talented artist. I think it is quite probable that in his retirement he might have dabbled with water colours or oil paints. If it pressed the right creative buttons for him, then he may have been satisfied to spend his days as an artist.

This about as far as logical probability goes, anything further is going to be pure speculation or more likely guesswork. I don't think it would help to try to predict what Edward and his family would do with the rest of their lives. They had already done enough.

THE ANALYTICAL ENGINE

Nowhere in the Optics Notebook does it mention the name, Charles Babbage and his difference engine. This suggests that Edward didn't know the gentleman concerned, and didn't know the nature of his work. It seems that the Admiralty didn't know either, or were making sure that they didn't meet.

Charles Babbage was primarily an extra-ordinary, gifted mathematician and polymath, with wide ranging interests in a huge variety of fields. If we are allowed to criticise him, it would be that he lacked mental discipline. He touched on so many fields, but mastered few. He produced countless erudite papers and books on everything from philosophy, religion, engineering, computation and medicine. Unlike Edward, who knew his limitations only too well and generally kept within the fields that he knew about. Edward was driven by practicality, whereas this was apparently of little interest to Babbage. They were two very different people; Babbage was independently wealthy whereas Edward worked for his living. Babbage was difficult and often secretive and obtuse, whereas Edward was affable, gentle and open-minded.

Charles Babbage announced his invention in June 1822 in a paper to the Royal Astronomical Society entitled 'Note on the application of machinery to the computation of astronomical and mathematical tables'. If the title had been a Nautical Almanac machine, then the Admiralty would have taken notice, but it wasn't.

Parliament certainly knew about Babbage because they authorised a spending budget of £1700 to fund the building of his difference engine. Babbage did produce a small working model in 1832. His initial design was a Colossus (15 tons weight and 8 feet tall), but the working model was built to 1/7th scale. Why such a strange scale? If it worked at 1/7th scale then why not scale down the whole thing? Parliament first suspended the project in 1833. This was public money after all and had to be justified.

The Treasury eventually lost patience and interest and the project was finally abandoned in 1842. By this time Babbage had managed to spend £17000, and still he had nothing to show for it. Babbage then went on to improve the design of the difference engine to become an analytical engine, which instantly made the difference engine obsolete. The analytical engine contained all the essential elements of a modern electronic computer, but in mechanical form. This feat speaks volumes about the creative abilities of Charles Babbage.

The Science Museum in London financed the construction of a difference engine in the year 2000 to Babbage's original No 2 design and using 19th century

179

technology, to celebrate the 200th anniversary of Babbage's birth. To date, nobody has attempted to construct an analytical engine, which was even bigger.

Babbage also invented an ophthalmoscope, which the medical profession ignored. The same instrument was again re-invented in 1851 by Herman von Helmholtz with much greater success.

Edward wasn't interested in calculating tables, instead his interest would have been breaking codes by machines. If machines could work quickly enough, then it might be possible to use a mathematical method to break a code, just by waiting long enough for the machine to produce a recognisable word. A difference engine would not have been much use in this context, but the analytical machine certainly had potential, because it could be programmed. Indeed, the first program written for the analytical engine was written in 1842 by Ada Lovelace, daughter of Lord Byron.

One area that Babbage touched on was cryptography, which Edward would have been keen to discuss with Babbage. They would have agreed on the weakness of substitution cyphers, which Edward had already solved by cleverly defeating letter frequency analysis, simply by changing the code with every letter, with a geared ratchet. Babbage on the other hand did some profound work on the use of 'keywords', particularly the use of Vigenère cyphers. Edward didn't use keywords, but in effect his code discs were the equivalent. Edward's scrambling device was effectively a very simple mechanical way of generating random keywords. Babbage even worked out how to break the Vigenère keyword cyphers by 1851, which would have interested Edward enormously. Both Edward and Babbage recognized that complex methods of coding and decoding had severe practical limitations unless it was done by machine. To his credit, Edward's methods were extremely simple and very secure, more importantly, he had already solved the mechanical issues.

It is interesting that both the difference engine and Edward's de-coding machines had built-in printers, but for different reasons; Babbage wanted to eliminate type-setting errors, whereas Edward just wanted to make the messages readable.

The two never met. I suppose in a way, this is not so surprising, because the very nature of anything to do with cryptography is 'sensitive' and likely to be secret. Indeed, the work that Babbage did, remained a secret until 1985, more than a century later. There is no way of knowing what might have happened if the two gentlemen had collaborated. Edward was the master of small, ingenious and elegance, and Babbage was clearly the master of theory, principle and scope.

At one time, the reason given for abandoning the difference engine project was that engineering accuracy in Babbage's day was not up to the task. Try telling that to Edward. Later when a full-scale model was made for the Science Museum, this fallacy was exposed.

Let us digress for a moment to consider the possibility that the Admiralty did know of Charles Babbage and that they did understand that the difference engine could also produce flawless and very accurate Nautical tables. This would be the Holy Grail for the Navy. Perhaps they struck a deal with Babbage, similar to the deal with Edward, that they would arrange funding to build his infernal machine in exchange for rights to the nautical tables, and some help with breaking coded messages. They could certainly make such a deal because they had great influence in Parliament.

For Charles Babbage this would have been a very tempting offer, which I have no doubt that he would have accepted, even if he quibbled about rights to his tables.

The Admiralty now had the problem of keeping Edward and Charles apart. Edward was no problem. He was driven by completing a task on time, doing it well, and getting paid for it. Charles on the other hand was independently wealthy, difficult to deal with, and ill disciplined. In modern parlance he was something of a loose cannon. Charles also knew many powerful and influential people.

Let us assume that the Admiralty were convinced that they could contain Charles, and confine him to developing his difference engine, and periodically give him samples of Edward's coded messages to see if he could unravel them using his ingenious mathematical methods. The ultimate benefits would be a set of flawless nautical tables, better than any other nation, and a testing ground for Edward's 'unbreakable' codes.

There would have been an endless daily supply of coded, printed paper tapes from the optical telegraph, so Charles would have no complaints about insufficient examples. I think it is reasonable to assume that Charles would have noticed that the paper tapes were printed and therefore were probably made by a machine. Had he been beaten to it? Did the Admiralty already have a difference engine or something like it? Had he been bought off to keep him quiet? Who knows what Charles would be thinking.

The next thing that he would have noticed is that the messages did not respond to letter frequency analysis. They were infinitely more complex than simple substitution. If the coding system was driven by keywords as used in Vigenère cyphers, there was no sign of keywords anywhere. He obviously noticed that many tapes had a different serial numbers on the header line, which he probably interpreted as being numeric references to a pre-arranged list of keywords. Without keywords he couldn't use his modular arithmetic to unravel the tapes, at least not without a difference engine, and even then the engine would need to be more sophisticated. An analytical engine perhaps? Maybe this would account for Charles developing the notion of an analytical engine and losing interest in the difference engine. Babbage never did build his analytical engine.

If Babbage had been really smart, he would have noticed that the tiny punched holes in the paper tape were based on binary notation. There was clearly much more to this code than was immediately obvious. Just by counting the different printed symbols he would have known that there were 31 characters. Simple substitution was not the answer and neither were Vigenère cyphers. Had he known about Edward's scrambling device, he could have quickly created a mathematical equivalent. With the aid of a machine, Babbage could have tried all the possible scrambling combinations until he came up with some recognizable words. The problem was that he didn't know about the scrambling device and he didn't have a machine either. Babbage was at the bottom of a very deep hole with no obvious way out.

Meanwhile, Edward continued to receive encouragement and praise for the simplicity of his devices and for the procedures that he had set out to ensure complete security, i.e. restricting access to the coding and de-coding devices and only using coded paper tapes between source and destination. He received no complaints about whether his codes were unbreakable or not.

Charles, on the other hand, has worries of his own. He kept getting endless examples of printed coded tapes that had obviously been produced by unknown machinery. Worse still, these codes did not respond to the usual methods of breaking codes. What he really needed was a translation of one or more tapes so that he could back-track to find out how the code was constructed and worked. This would not have gone down well with the Admiralty. Since when does the enemy give you clues to its cyphers? Besides, they already knew how Edward's system worked, because they were using it every day.

What mattered to the Admiralty was whether the codes were breakable or not. Was Edward correct in his analysis that very sophisticated codes would take too long to break, and were effectively unbreakable for this reason? The results from Charles Babbage were buried in incomprehensible mathematical rhetoric, but at the end of the day his comments were inconclusive. By default, Edward's view prevailed.

The Admiralty was not composed of men with infinite patience. At some stage their patience would and did run out. They pulled the plug on Charles. No doubt they were a trifle annoyed at not getting their improved nautical tables, but for the moment they could at least depend on Edward's unbreakable codes. Perhaps this is the reason why the Navy persisted with the optical telegraph for so long after its sell-by-date. Even after the change to an electric telegraph, we know that the coders and de-coders were still being used, because the Notebook tells us so.

This is a very plausible explanation for the recorded facts at the time. The Admiralty may have been composed of a very large number of ageing admirals and vice-admirals, but they were not stupid. They could certainly recognise genius when they saw it, and they knew how to put it to good use.

From The Admiralty's point of view, the change to an electric telegraph provided by the General Post Office, brought the cost of sending messages tumbling down. They only had to pay for the time taken to send each message, rather than paying for an exclusive telegraph that worked around the clock. The downside was that the electric telegraph was a 'public' service rather than a private service. However, this was not a problem for the Navy, because their messages would be in secret code that was essentially unbreakable, as far as they knew.

THE WOKING BREAK

Saturday, 9 August 1828
Jerry was in my office when I arrived. Urgent message from
Weybridge says line is broken at Woking. Operator travelled to
Weybridge by mail coach to give warning. Instantly wrote
grateful reply to Weybridge and gave to Jerry to send. Asked
Jimmy to get a carter to take 2-mile bobbin and 4 men to
Weybridge. Then trace break back towards Woking. Connect
new cable. Test it works then hang cable on wire between posts.
(S) packed lunch. 10 am carter and team left for Weybridge –
aim to arrive tomorrow.

The Workshop notebook was hardly a meteorological diary, but from time to time Edward noted the weather conditions, if he thought the telegraph cable might be at risk of damage. On 9 August 1828 a severe gale struck London and the south-east causing much property damage, including the Portsmouth cable. An elm tree had been up-rooted and fell across the cable, breaking the support wire, about 3 miles south of Weybridge. The weight of the tree had bent the cable around too small a radius and this had fractured the glass filaments.

The operator on duty at Woking, bravely stopped a passing mail coach and paid the coachman to take her to the next repeater station at Weybridge (7 miles distance). It was this station that sent an emergency message to Edward, which was intercepted by Jerry

Ballard at Kennington, who immediately rode to Leadenhall Street. He was waiting in Edward's office, drinking tea, when Edward arrived for work.

Edward immediately spoke to Jimmy to hire his most reliable carter to pick up a replacement cable bobbin and four men (including Jimmy) to travel to Weybridge, and then to follow the cable line until they reached the break. The team should then trace back the nearest couplings either side of the break and should then connect the replacement cable. Initially they should lay the cable on the ground and only when they were certain that the line was working, should they raise the cable to the supporting wire. Sybil gave Jimmy sufficient money to compensate the operator at Woking for the cost of the journey to Weybridge. She also packed bread, cheese and some bottled ale for lunch on the way.

Edward then composed a message of gratitude for the vigilance of the Woking operator and that she would be compensated. A replacement cable was already on its way and should arrive in two days. He gave this message to Jerry to send to the Weybridge station.

Within minutes a carter arrived in the back yard and the spare 2-mile bobbin was hoisted onboard together with the four passengers. Jimmy was given charge of the 'purse' that contained sufficient money for food and lodgings for the team and the 'driver'. The journey to

Weybridge was about 25 miles, and at that time a horse could only be driven 20 miles in a day. The men could have been sent by mail chaise to Weybridge in about 4 hours, but they could do nothing without the replacement cable.

Monday, 11 August 1828

Jimmy returned this evening with repair team. Very proud of their efforts. Jerry already knows repair is working. Carter stopped horses half way to Weybridge for rest. Arrived Ship Inn same day. Searched for cable break. Found break at fallen Elm tree 3 miles south of Weybridge. Cut tree in pieces and dragged clear with horses. Replaced cable at nearest couplings. Went to Woking to confirm line was working. Collected old cable. Hung new cable on wire. Ship Inn for night, then early start to London. Rest half way as before. Arrived London same evening. Jimmy suggests sending bobbins to remote stations for storage. In future on long journeys send men by mail coach and pick up bobbins at nearest station.

According to Jimmy, the carter stopped about half way to Weybridge to rest the horses and let them graze, while the team and the carter enjoyed a lunch break. After lunch most of the team walked for a few miles to lighten the load, but it started to rain so they took cover in the wagon. Resting the horses at the half way point, enabled them to complete the journey to The Ship Inn at Weybridge by sunset. After a good meal the team decided to have a drink or two, while Jimmy went looking for the repeater station. He found it quite easily, because it was the only premises illuminated by candles at this time of night. He knocked on the door and announced who he was and the reason for his visit. He asked the duty operator to send an un-coded message to Edward, telling him the team were already in Weybridge for the night.

The following day, Jimmy took it upon himself to be the foreman and directed the carter to walk the horses, following the line of the cable until they spotted the break, about 3 miles south of the repeater station. It wasn't a true break, like the supporting wire: the cable was just drooping between the posts. Closer examination revealed that the telegraph cable had been bent around a very tight radius and the glass rods within had been shattered. The horses were stopped, and Jimmy sent two of the team backwards and forwards to the two nearest coupling joints.

The rest of the team set about the offending Elm tree with axes until the pieces were small enough to be dragged clear by the horses.

When the coupling points had been located, the carter drove on to the most forward joint where they manhandled the bobbin of cable from the wagon. The existing joint was un-coupled, and the new cable was connected. Slowly they rolled the bobbin along the road, carefully laying the cable beneath the existing cable. The nearest joint to Weybridge was then uncoupled and the end of the new cable was added in its place.

The carter then took them into Woking to check if the line was working, and to pay the operator for the mail coach ride. Jimmy asked for a message to be sent to Edward to confirm that the line was fully functional. It was around midday now, so the carter took them back to pick up the damaged cable and to re-hang the new cable on the support wire. The old cable was rewound onto the wooden bobbin and then the team retired to the Ship Inn to rest for the night.

At dawn the next day they all set off back to London, with a similar stop about half way to rest the horses, and by evening the team were back in their own homes. Edward and Jerry were both impressed by the speed that the broken cable had been replaced, and that the telegraph was functioning properly. Edward reminded Jerry how important it had been to be able to contact his operators. Jimmy politely reminded Edward that perhaps he should think about keeping spare bobbins at appropriate locations along each of the routes, because in some cases breakdowns in the more remote stations could take much longer to travel to and fix.

THE HASLEMERE SQUIRRELS

Wednesday, 1 October 1834

In the afternoon Jerry arrived with an urgent message from the Milford station. The operator at Haslemere had walked the 6 miles to Milford to report a line fault. Jerry didn't seem too concerned because London was enveloped in thick fog since yesterday, which paralysed the city. I sent a message to Milford saying that were on our way and should arrive in two days with a replacement cable. I knew that Weybridge had a spare bobbin and that the repair team could easily get to Weybridge in a day (usually). The fog might cause some delay. I decided to join the team because I wanted to be away from the fog. Jerry offered to send a rider to warn (E). We spent the night at the Ship Inn and the following day I hired a carter to take us the 30 miles south to Haslemere. We followed the cable route from Milford to Haslemere and were almost in the town when Jimmy spotted a frayed section of cable near a stand of conifers just before St. Bartholemews church, which is a short walk to the Haslemere station in the High Street. The cable had been chewed by some animals. There was no cotton binding over a 4 foot section, and the Shola had been chewed away, exposing the glass filaments. Two of the filaments were broken. Jimmy asked local residents what they thought. Apparently the stand of trees was home to several red squirrels, who had been seen walking the cable. It was a simple task to connect the new cable to Haslemere station and the next joint towards Milford. We didn't collect the old cable. Instead we mounted the new cable 4 inches below, but still using the same wire. This allowed the squirrels to continue using the top cable as a walk-way. The town boast a good brass band but not enough time to stay and listen. I like brass brands and piano recitals, but not choral works. Back home two days later by mail coach. Still thick fog in London. (E) and children very happy (M) too.

There is little to add to Edward's full account of this incident. I think that he made a wise decision to leave the old cable in place, which allowed the squirrels to continue using the cable as a means of traversing to the nearest downward support post. Placing the new cable immediately below the old one, would probably discourage the squirrels from attempting to use the new cable. It could be said that the broken glass ends would be a hazard to wild life, but at that time, wild life protection was not on the agenda.

On another note entirely, Edward admits to liking brass bands and piano recitals, but not choral music. This is the first mention of any interest in music.

There are no other references to problems with the cable at Haslemere, so it seems the squirrels were content with the new arrangements.

According to weather records of the time, there was a period of continuous fog in London between 30 September to 6 October. Jerry was right not to be too concerned about the short interruption to the telegraph service. There was no fog at the farmhouse, but the view from the hill showed a distinct fog layer over the city.

The railways were spreading across the nation at this time like a plague, but there is no mention of rail travel in this episode. Clearly the railways were not going to places that Edward needed to visit.

Curiously, Edward refers to Peter and Amy as the children, because Peter was 15 years old and Amy was 14 years old. On the other hand, at that time minors did not become adults until the age of 21 years old, so perhaps Edward can be forgiven for calling them children.

Looking back through the Notebook, there is no mention of illness by any member of the 'family'. At least nobody complained about it. London, like all big urban centres had more than its fair share of epidemics that killed off thousands, but it seems that Edward and his family escaped them all. I would guess that they must have had bouts of the common cold and probably headaches too, and possibly mild stomach upsets, but nothing worthy of a mention in the Notebook.

I would put this down to a clean water supply, fresh milk, and a pollution free atmosphere (Norwood was essentially rural at that time). I also get the impression that Edward and Elsie were particular about personal hygiene, which would have reduced the risk of infection. We also know that Edward was obsessive about safety, so it would have been unlikely that the children would have experienced broken bones. The family enjoyed a good diet of fresh vegetables and fruit in season, and there is no mention of sugar in any form in the Notebook. There is no mention of dental care either. Perhaps the family were blessed with good, strong teeth, or maybe the spring water contained traces of fluorides.

One way or another the family escaped serious illness. Mary, in particular, survived child birth twice, and her children both survived beyond the age of five. For the times, this was an achievement, because death in child birth and infant mortality rates were very high.

THE DARMOOR INCIDENT

Saturday, 20 January 1838
Urgent message from Totnes, Devon, delivered by rider from
Kennington. South Brent station reports line is down.
Instantly warned Jerry of line breakage at South Brent station.
Jerry not concerned. Fierce storm so no ships docking at
Devonport or Falmouth. Immediately booked 4 men (including
Jimmy) to travel by mail coach to Newton Abbot which is
where nearest bobbin is stored.

Dartmoor ponies have lived in a semi-feral state on Dartmoor for thousands of years. Its size (12 hands) and strength make it an ideal workhorse for the local tin mines. Usually they forage for food on the moors, but when the weather conditions are particularly severe they tend to stray wider. Such an event occurred a few days before and after 20 January 1838, when the temperature at Greenwich dropped to minus 16 Celsius. The temperature on the moors was probably even less, accompanied by considerable snow. A herd of ponies made for the southern edge of the moors near to the South Brent repeater station, where the support posts had been loosened by a very wet summer the year before, causing the cable to droop and obstruct the path of the ponies. The ponies trampled on the cable over a short stretch and severed the Devonport line. This interruption was reported immediately by the Totnes station who were suspicious that no messages were being sent, and the operator at South Brent was not responding to the 'Ready' or 'Send' signals.

The nearest reserve bobbin was kept at the Newton Abbot station, but it would take the repair team between two and three days by mail chaise to collect the spare bobbin and another day to locate the break and repair it.

To her credit, one of the operators from South Brent ventured out in the appalling weather and walked along the line and located the break just over a mile towards Totnes. A passing farmer took her aboard his wagon to the Totnes station to pass on this information. By this time, the repair team were about to depart for the mail coach to Exeter.

Jerry, at the Admiralty, didn't seem too concerned about the interruption to the Devonport service. If the weather was as bad as had been reported, then very few ships would be arriving or leaving Falmouth or Devonport. He knew that the repairs were in competent hands and was prepared to wait.

Tuesday, 23 January 1838
Message from Jimmy at South Brent station. Line repaired. Had to un-freeze cable overnight at blacksmith's forge. Also used kettles of hot water. Dreadful weather. Wild Dartmoor ponies trampled on cable. Local people very helpful. Generous with scrumpy. Tell Sally I am back in 3-4 days.

Four days later, South Brent reported that the line was fully operational again. During its lifetime (30 years), the cable only suffered three interruptions; Woking, Haslemere and South Brent. Edward and the whole firm were exceedingly proud of this record.

The repair team arrived back at the workshop with exaggerated tales of their battle with the elements. It seems it was so cold that it was difficult to unwind the new bobbin of cable. In the end they paid the blacksmith at Totnes to gently thaw out the bobbin close to his forge overnight. Even so, they still had to pour kettles of hot water over parts of the cable so that it became supple enough to uncoil. At least the team were unanimous in their praise for the hospitality of the local people and the copious supplies of 'scrumpy' (coarse cider).

It is amazing to think that a simple idea in 1816 lasted for about 30 years, virtually without modification. A fitting tribute to Victorian engineering or perhaps we should say Georgian engineering and ingenuity.

BEGINNING OF THE END

Edward's visionary dream of a nation wide optical telegraph was doomed centuries before he even started his work for the Admiralty. Back in 1643 the first Post Office was opened in London in Cloak Lane, originally intended for carrying Royal messages, but was later extended to the public. The Royal Mail was essentially a monopoly, legally approved by the government of the day to carry messages from the sender to the receiver. A magnificent, purpose-built facility was erected between 1825 and 1829, at St Martins Le Grand. Over time four additional branch offices were built in the City. Later still, in 1870 a Telegraph department was added nearby. In 1910, the headquarters was moved to the King Edward building.

The key point was that the General Post Office was a state monopoly with respect to sending and receiving messages regardless of the means; whether it was by mail, electric telegraph, optical telegraph, radio or electronic means. The Post Office claimed them all. Initially there were several private companies who had developed different types of electric telegraph and telephone systems, but these were all taken over by the Post Office, backed up by various Acts of Parliament.

Eventually, the monopoly caught up with Edward's optical telegraph. In 1869 the Telegraph Act was passed, which allowed the Post Office to acquire all inland telegraph operations. By this time electric telegraph systems had become the Post Office standard, largely due to the massive expansion of the railway network across the nation, carrying electric cables alongside the rail tracks.

In December 1878 the Post Office obtained a court judgement that telephone conversations fell within the Telegraph Act and promptly entered the 'phone business, again as a monopoly. Later, in 1904, under the Wireless Telegraphy Act, radio transmission came within the scope of the Post Office, which also included television broadcasting.

Friday, 7 May 1847.
Summoned to Admiralty. Closure of Optical Telegraph announced in favour of electric telegraph. Very sad, after 30 years faithful and reliable service. Like a death in the family, but the signs were clear that this would happen. Collected all equipment. Put in store in Kennington. Perhaps donate to museum. Business revenue now seriously reduced. (S) tells workers to look for jobs. Instrument business in serious decline. Many in trade now bankrupt. Humidors still good, oil fillers, Shola paper, good but for how long? Designed brass cylinder rule (Accurus), but few orders. Moved all equipment from next door so rent reduced. Salvaged as much as possible. Not much value there except comp air engines. Brass name plates worth a tidy sum. Good investment. Suddenly remembered a steam

omnibus ride some 5 years ago Paddington to Islington . Did experiments with hair fine filaments but still need strong light. Still have Admiralty commission. Helping with change to electric cable. Intend to do away with paper tape. Not good idea. Could survive with ease on savings and lieutenant's pay. (E) (M) and children safe. (S) safe too. Probably shut down business in 5 to 10 years. So sad to see so many wonderful and skilled people going. Take a holiday with (E) and (M) and children. Give brain a rest. Perhaps new ideas will come again.

Edward and the Admiralty were not immediately affected, and the semaphore line (or more probably the optical cable) continued to operate successfully for almost 30 years until 1847. The Admiralty eventually decided to move with the times and up-dated their communications to an all-weather, day and night electric cable, that didn't need human repeater stations.

Following the demise of the optical cable business, Edward did his best to keep the firm afloat. Sadly, the instrument business had gone into serious decline over the past thirty years, but the firm still had the craftsmen that could produce accurate instruments, so Edward designed an extremely accurate slide rule; a device that he had used all his life. His cylindrical rule was equivalent to a six feet long straight rule, even though the cylinder was only 12-inches long. It was also equipped with a Vernier magnifier for even greater accuracy. He called his instrument 'The Accurus'. It was made in solid brass and the scales were engraved by hand. Ayres and Compton would have been proud of this magnificent device in its mahogany box. Despite its accuracy the device did not sell as well as Edward hoped.

At the suggestion from Sybil, Edward had already removed all the glass cable production equipment from the premises next door, so they were no longer paying the rent. His workmen salvaged as much as they could from the process line, including the tiny pneumatic engines. He even contemplated producing these compressed air engines in bulk, but at that time very few firms had sufficient compressed air capacity. Much later in the century the Admiralty did use compressed air engines to propel torpedoes.

Sybil also warned all the workmen that the collapse of the optical telegraph had thrown the company into a very difficult financial situation. They would be well advised to look for alternative employment. She reminded Edward that he still had a commission with the Navy which would probably last until he retired provided he continued to keep to his contract. In fact, Edward was keeping to his contract by assisting with the change over to electric cables. Initially, his coding and decoding machines continued in operation, but he was informed that eventually these would be replaced and that paper tapes would cease to be used. Edward disapproved of this move, but he was no longer in a position of any influence in these matters.

When all the repeater station premises were closed. Edward had the brass name plates removed and these sold well for a tidy profit, because they could be melted down and re-used.

One item that was selling well was the lamp-oil filler, but Edward was aware, that his version was made by craftsmen in brass. It wouldn't take somebody long to work out how to make a can in steel by machine. Anyone who could make 'tin cans' could also make oil fillers.

The lens grinders were still reasonably busy making specialist lenses, but there were countless others in the same business. Long term continuity was unlikely.

The shola pith paper making machine was still operational and some glass makers were still buying these packing sheets, but there was no way of knowing how long this would last.

Edward also carried out experiments with hair fine filaments of glass gathered together as a cord or rope. He attached a lens at one end and a microscope at the other, and was surprised that the image was so good, provided it was strongly illuminated. Vulcanized rubber had been patented in America shortly before this time but was not available in a form that Edward could use to coat his flexible glass rope, so Edward discarded his idea. The medical profession had to wait until the new century before a practical endoscope was produced.

A strong light source still eluded Edward, so there was little chance of developing a commercial, nation-wide optical cable. Even if he did find a solution, there was every chance that the General Post Office would buy him out and shut down his operation in favour of the electric telegraph. Whichever way he turned, Edward was confronted with obstacles for which there was no immediate solution.

Some five years earlier, Edward had travelled from Paddington to Islington aboard a steam powered omnibus, called 'The Enterprise', built by Walter Handcock. He was impressed by the sturdiness and reliability of the vehicle but was critical of its steam power. He considered that it would be far safer to use compressed air. He recalled thinking at the time that perhaps this was a vision of the future. As usual, Edward was thinking a few years ahead of the times. Thirty years later Mekarski air powered trams travelled the streets of Paris and elsewhere for more than 30 years.

Probably for the first time in his life, Edward was confronted by a dismal picture of the future. Even the weather, that year, was exceedingly dismal. At least he had the girls and the children for comfort. Many in this cruel world were far worse off than he.

Thursday, 25 November 1858
Business closed down (not bankrupt). Closed doors for last time.
Cried quietly. (S) too. (E) and (M) cried for me.

The two senior partners, Ayres and Compton, had long since passed away, leaving Edward as the lone surviving partner. The firm's major source of revenue virtually disappeared over night when the Admiralty changed to the electric telegraph. The company still made humidors and other high-quality cabinets, but this was insufficient to keep the company afloat. The company doors were eventually shut for the last time in November 1858 when Edward retired.

Edward was obviously sad to see the demise of his optical cable, but at least it had brought prosperity to the company for almost half a century. Understandably, Edward didn't want all his equipment to be destroyed, so he purchased, for a song, what he could at Admiralty auctions and put it all into store along with spare bobbins of cable. He may have intended to donate this collection to a museum, but never got around to the task. His collection remained in store beyond his death for half a century. Presumably, Elsie or Amy or the grandchildren continued to pay storage fees, rather than part with these mementoes of Edward.

On 15 October 1940, just after 8:00 pm a bombing raid by the Luftwaffe, destroyed a large area of Kennington, including a civilian air-raid shelter, killing approximately 104 people (not all the bodies were recovered). Nearby was a small storage building containing the remains of Edward's optical cable collection, which was totally obliterated. Nothing was recovered. The only object to survive, to mark Edward's achievement was his Workshop Notebook. Presumably, it was in Amy's personal possession (or more likely, her children) at the time.

I recall from my childhood that it was customary in early September (at the beginning of the school year) to cover all textbooks issued by the school, in brown paper, to extend the life expectancy of the textbook. At some point, the Workshop Notebook received this same treatment. Inadvertently, the book was turned over and re-labelled on the wrong cover. At first glance this now appeared to be an empty, unused book, because the neatly written contents were only written on one side of each page.

Friday 22 April 1859
Final entry. Spring has arrived. Warm spell. Have arranged to take a very long holiday in West country with (E) and (M). The children are both happy and secure. Everyone is so excited. Packing trunks. Immense sense of relief. Best decision to spend more time with girls and visits from the children and grandma. A very good life so far. Looking forwards to doing it all again. Love them all so much.

ABOUT THE AUTHOR

J. Randolf Scott, a retired Chemical Engineer, and father of five children, lives in the heart of rural England with his youngest daughter. A prolific inventor and innovator, the author is also an artist and a Fellow of the Institution of Analysts and Programmers. In his own words, "As an artist I paint what I see, and in my books I paint in words what I see in my mind". During his career he has travelled to most countries in the world, and this is reflected in the scope and subject matter of his writing. His novels cover a wide range of genres, from thrillers, to period romance and science fiction, and he admits that background research often takes much longer than writing the novel itself, particularly in this book.

Printed in Great Britain
by Amazon

50377636R00120